The Underground Press in America

Frontispiece

PLATE 1 *Perhaps the major contribution of the underground press to newspaper graphics has been psychedelic art. This page from the San Francisco Oracle (February 1967, p. 20) was printed with a bleed of blue and yellow-green inks over a purple design, and is characteristic of the visions of artists who have been influenced by psychedelic drugs. [Printed with permission of the Oracle]*

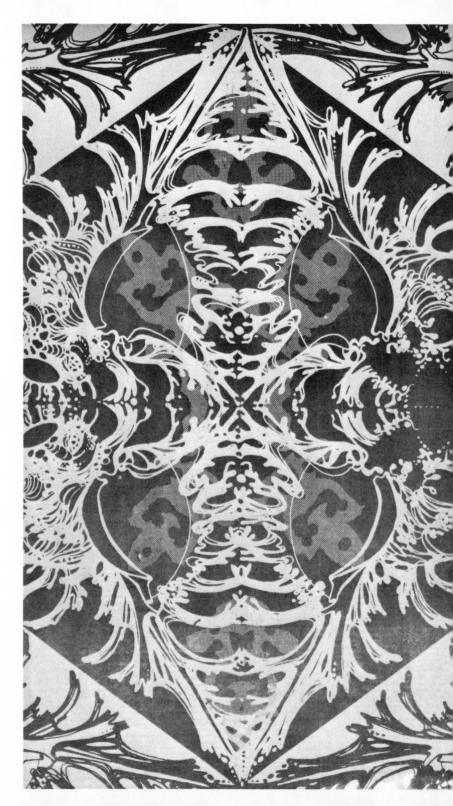

The Underground Press

in America

by Robert J. Glessing

GREENWOOD PRESS, PUBLISHERS
WESTPORT, CONNECTICUT

Library of Congress Cataloging in Publication Data

Glessing, Robert J.
   The underground press in America.

   Reprint. Originally published: Bloomington : Indiana
University Press, 1970.
   Includes bibliographical references and index.
   1. Underground press--United States. I. Title.
PN4888.U5G5 1984   071'.3   84-6521
ISBN 0-313-24450-2 (lib. bdg.)

Reprinted in 1984 by Greenwood Press
A division of Congressional Information Service, Inc.
88 Post Road West, Westport, Connecticut 06881

Printed in the United States of America

10 9 8 7 6 5 4 3 2 1

To Bob Dylan

who did the lonely groundwork

to show America where it was at

Contents

FUTURE / Where It's Going

Preface

WHEN THIS WRITER WAS A HIGH SCHOOL STUDENT in Syracuse, New York, Syracuse University football games were the social highlights of the fall season. Since the price of tickets was out of reach for most south side gang kids, ingenuity had to substitute for money in getting in to view the autumnal madness. One method was for nine or ten kids to go in together, indicating to the ticket-taker in hitchhiking fashion with their thumbs that the person behind had the tickets. Of course none of us had tickets but by the time that was detected, six or seven would be dispersed inside the crowded stadium. If the ticket-taker pursued any of the ones who had got in, those in the rear of the line would rush past the unattended gate.

This book has been put together in a similar way. In one sense the many underground reporters, editors and students who patiently, and often articulately explained their role in the development of the Underground press in America, "had the tickets."

Underground editors and staffers were especially generous with their time and opinions and added greatly to any perspective the reader might gain from this book. Among the many, particular thanks go to Tom Forcade (Underground Press Syndicate), Allan Katzman (*East Village Other*), John Wilcock (*Other Scenes*), Paul Krassner (*Realist*), Sheila Grant (Berkeley *Tribe*), Jeff Shero and Jon Grell (*Rat*), Marvin Garson and Doc Stanley (*Good Times*), Ed Fancher (*Village Voice*), Bill Biggins (*Philadelphia Free Press*), Bill Rowe (*Fifth Estate*), Clark Smith (*The Ally*), Ted Zatlyn (*Los Angeles Free Press*), James Ridgeway (*Hard Times*), Joe

Blum, Lincoln and Arlene Bergman (*The Movement*), Terry Sebella (*Seed*), Margie Stamberg (*The Guardian*), John Bryan (*Open City*), Allan Cohen (*San Francisco Oracle*), and Walter Wells (*The Illustrated Paper*).

Paul Slater and Richard Bradshaw, two California graduate students who were completing thesis studies on the underground press at the time this manuscript was being prepared, contributed considerably to the research, and Richard Adler, a member of the English Department of the University of California at Berkeley, gave generously of his time and offered many helpful suggestions on revising the original text.

This book was largely written and researched during a summer reprieve from teaching at Cañada College in Redwood City, California. Any shortcomings in scope, errors in fact, or misjudgments in interpretation are solely due to the author's limitations in time and talent, not to the above-mentioned persons.

The book would not and could not have been written but for my wife, Martha Meinert Glessing, and Michael Aronson, formerly assistant director at Indiana University Press, who more than any others believed in and encouraged the recording of this brief history of the new medium.

ROBERT J. GLESSING

Introduction

FOR THE MOST PART, PROFESSIONAL JOURNALISTS AND journalism educators have brushed the Underground Press aside as a passing fad—too obscene and too irresponsible to merit close examination. The truth of the matter is, however, that the Underground Press typifies a new brand of journalism in the making. It holds the possibility of initiating changes just as significant as those introduced at earlier critical junctures in the history of journalism— that is, the advent of the Party Press, The Penny Press, Yellow Journalism, and even the electronic media.

Each of those journalistic watersheds has coincided—in fact, in large measure resulted from—one or all of a number of forces at work in the society: (1) technological advancements, (2) political upheaval, (3) anti-establishment movements, and (4) social-intellectual change. The Penny Press, for example, would have been impossible without the Industrial Revolution. It brought the application of steam power to printing presses and made mass production of newspapers selling at a penny each possible for the first time in history. The lure of the growing industrial cities, fed from rural populations being displaced by labor-saving farm equipment, provided a ready market for the new, cheap press. The specialization of labor and mass production of goods resultant from the Industrial Revolution furnished the basis for advertising support of the media. Slum conditions, labor unrest, and the general unsettling conditions accompanying industrialization stimulated editorials and newspaper campaigns in behalf of the rising urban masses. And the spread of literacy and universal suffrage helped build a large, politically-aware audience.

The unique new press that emerged from these various socio-economic circumstances proved to be violently anti-establishment at certain points and, considering the mores of the times, just as offensive to polite society as today's Underground Press. For instance, James Gordon Bennett, an iconoclast who founded the *New York Herald,* delighted in shocking readers by referring to legs instead of limbs, shirts instead of linens, and pantaloons instead of unmentionables. He was just as irreverent of the religious community. On one occasion he declared: "I don't think much of Moses. A man who would take forty years to get a party of people through a desert is only a loafer." On another occasion he wrote of the Roman Catholic doctrine of transubstantiation: "The ancient Egyptians worshipped the ox, bull, and crocodile. Yet they had not discovered the taste, as we Catholics have done, of making a God out of bread and adoring and eating him at the same time."

The very same forces that marked journalistic watersheds such as the Penny Press can be found in the American social milieu today. Most of them are already at work on the Underground Press and just may make it a signal factor in a new kind of journalism. From its outset, for example, the Underground Press has latched onto modern technical inventions, and in the process contradicted a well-worn dogma of Twentieth Century journalism. That is, for decades observers of the mass media have contended that the dissenter, the little man, the innovator, cannot possibly find an outlet for his views because of the prohibitive cost of starting and maintaining competition with the established, generally-conservative status quo press. Offset printing, justifying typewriters, and camera-ready copy processes disprove the theory and, in fact, reverse trends that only a decade ago seemed immutable. The whole history of the Underground Press is one of dissenters speaking out for political change and without fail damning the establishment. The advent of inexpensive new typesetting and printing processes—along with the Underground Press' disregard of union benefits and normal business practices—has helped give rebirth to the journalism of dissent.

Much like their journalistic predecessors, the essence of the questions being raised by today's underground are spiritual in nature. Today's youth may not be pious in the traditional sense, but they are spiritual in the way theologian Reinhold Neibuhr advocates. That is, they are asking the all-consuming questions of life: What is the nature of God? What is the nature of man's relationship to God and of man to man? They are asking, in the final analysis, what is the nature of justice. What is the nature of justice in Southeast Asia? What is the nature of jusice in the ghetto? What is the nature of justice in race relations?

Once again youth have turned to the Underground Press because they have found treatment by the professional and regular scholastic press inadequate. The underground movement has responded by editorializing on civil rights, social welfare, colonialism, flower children, international peace movements, and the inhumanity of war.

Finally, the Underground Press is in part a reaction to the social phenomenon of declining individualism in this country. Young people in particular have resented this trend. Not only the growing megapolis and the expanding corporation, but also particularly the consolidated school, work against individualism. Thirty to forty thousand students thrown together on some of the massive campuses in the country became lost in a maze of red tape, bureaucratic structure, and impersonal rules. Even high school students, now housed in complexes accommodating as many as five thousand students, find themselves little more than computer numbers.

Consequently, the Underground Press has found a ready market for its advocacy of long hair, Goodwill clothing, and other personal eccentricities. Its attacks on constraints of society and the conformity of big business have also fallen on receptive eyes.

The movement has not only editorialized strongly on behalf of "doing your own thing," but also has offered aspiring writers an opportunity to practice personal journalism. Art work, layout, design, content, and writing style reflect individualized approaches. In contrast to the growing trend toward group journalism in the news magazines and on the metropolitan newspapers, the Underground Press allows an individual personal involvement in every step of the journalistic process—from conceiving story ideas to pasting up camera-ready copy. In fact, necessity probably dictates that the underground journalist also take his own pictures, help with art work, even deliver the papers. The result is often a sense of dedication that high salaries could never buy, but that comes cheaply when an opportunity is provided for individual expression.

To explain some of the causal factors of the Underground Press is not necessarily to give a blanket endorsement of the movement. The Undeground Press does suffer from serious faults. For one thing, the underground papers openly practice deliberate bias as an integral part of their creed. The facts are often marshaled to fit the theory, whether or not they represent a full and balanced picture and whether or not they check out. Furthermore, known facts sometimes are deliberately withheld because they might contradict the theory. For another thing, many of the underground papers confuse rather than clarify because they fail to focus on given issues. Instead, free love, Vietnam, pollution, and the dirty speech movement are all mixed into the same article. Too often, none of the issues comes across with any depth or acumen.

Another criticism of underground papers concerns their indiscriminate employment of sexual materials and overindulgence in tasteless language. The obsession some have for using a half-dozen or so four-letter words raises not only questions of taste but even more serious doubts about the creative resources of their writers and editors. Journalists of dissent across the ages have been able to attack injustices in society without resorting to such low-level diction, and the results have been more efficacious than most yet produced by the current Underground Press.

Benjamin Franklin, who helped operate what was probably the first underground paper in America, employed wit and pure cleverness in drafting satirical letters against the establishment of his time. Writing under the pseudonym Silas Dogood, he produced in the early 1720s for his brother's paper, the *New England Courant*, a series of chatty epistles that poked fun and criticism at all manner of persons, customs, and institutions. When only seventeen, he chided the Boston elders about their propensity for titles and status—a complaint still popular among youth. Franklin wrote:

> *In old time it was no disrespect for men and women to be*
> *called by their own names. Adam was never called Master*
> *Adam; we never read of Noah Esquire, Lot Knight and Baronet,*
> *nor the Right Honourable Abraham, Viscount Mespotamia,*
> *Baron of Canaan. No, no, they were plain men, honest country*
> *graziers, that took care of their families and their flocks. Moses*
> *was a great prophet and Aaron a priest of the Lord; but we*
> *never read of the Reverend Moses nor the Right Reverend*
> *Father in God, Aaron, by Divine Providence Lord Archbishop*
> *of Israel. Thou never sawest Madam Rebecca in the Bible, my*
> *Lady Rachel; nor Mary, though a princess of the blood, after*
> *the death of Joseph called the Princess Dowager of Nazareth.*
> *No, plain Rebecca, Rachel, Mary, or the Widow Mary, or the*
> *like. It was no incivility then to mention their naked names as*
> *they were expressed.*

Franklin also had a talent for writing slogans, some of which have survived for almost 250 years now. His famous "Join or Die" editorial cartoon will, no doubt, outlast the "Bullshit" themes so widely displayed in the Underground Press today.

Whether any aspects of the Underground Press, let alone its slogans, will prove viable remains to be seen. It already has exhibited some strengths, however, including: (1) the ability to attract and hold youth while regular newspapers are floundering with that audience, (2) enough inventiveness in layout and design to influence the professional media, and (3) demonstrated ability to gain access for dissenters to the marketplace of ideas long after press experts had decreed the old libertarian principle dead.

That the movement has been subjected to severe attack despite these accomplishments is not at all surprising. The very first newspaper to appear in this country, *Publick Occurrences—Both Foreign and Domestick,* was banned after its initial issue because it carried criticism of the Colony's Indian affairs and a spicy item about an illicit relationship the French king had been carrying on with the prince's wife. The historical path of journalistic dissent has been littered with casualties ever since. But when journals of dissent have persisted and had something of genuine importance to say, they have overcome critical attacks, tar and feathers, and even death, to make a lasting imprint on society. Witness the eventual success of the Patriot Press of Samuel Adams and Thomas Paine in Revolutionary times and the Abolitionist Press of Horace Greeley and Elijah P. Lovejoy in the Civil War period. Sometimes journalists can overcome an early unsavory reputation and go on to win not only acceptance of their dissent but accolades from society and the journalistic profession. Joseph Pulitzer, for instance, who in the late 1800s was castigated for inventing most of the ills associated with the term "yellow journalist," reformed his newspapers to the point that his name now stands for the very highest standards of journalistic excellence.

The accomplishments of the current Underground Press remain to be recorded by future historians and press critics. The ensuing chapters by Robert Glessing should prove helpful in reaching that decision, for his is a pioneer effort in studying and assessing the Underground Press on a systematic basis.

RICHARD G. GRAY, *Chairman*

Department of Journalism
Indiana University

Past / *Where It's Been*

1 / An Overview

About the Book

I tell you the past is a bucket of ashes.
I tell you yesterday is a wind gone down,
a sun dropped in the west.

—CARL SANDBURG[1]

THE UNDERGROUND PRESS IN AMERICA WAS CREATED
to reflect and shape the life style of hippies, dropouts and all those
alienated from the mainstream of American experience. In one
sense it can be said that underground newspapers are written *by* the
alienated *for* the alienated. Weary of what the underground Boston
Avatar called "mindless mass journalism," estranged editors and
readers sought a more colorful alternative to the stereotyped, broadside, black-and-white overground press.

The contemporary term "underground press" stems from the
rush of anti-establishment newspapers in the early 1960s when most
underground papers reflected the American drug culture. Since
drugs were, and are, illegal, the name "underground press" caught
on and held.

When surveying the underground press in America it becomes
obvious that the directors of this new medium are themselves uncertain as to which publications are more and which less underground.
The *Guardian* in New York City claims it is not underground but,

rather, "radical." The *Movement*, a 20,000 circulation, twenty-four-page tabloid out of San Francisco, also disclaims the underground label and considers itself "revolutionary." The Los Angeles *Free Press*, one of the most prominent and successful of the underground papers, calls itself "the alternative press" and Ted Zatlyn, one of the *Freep*'s first editors insists, "We're a paper in radical evolution." Back east the *Village Voice*, which was founded by Norman Mailer in 1955 and considers itself the father of modern underground newspapers, is so widely patronized by big business that it refers to itself as the "Trendmaker" and appears to be very overground indeed! Comparing the *Village Voice* to Paul Krassner's *Realist*, one New York writer referred to the outrageously irreverent *Realist* as the "*Village Voice* with its fly open."[2] Krassner argues his publication is not underground either and that "the only underground newspaper in America is the *Outlaw* which is produced by the inmates of San Quentin prison." From the Underground Press Syndicate itself, the unofficial voice of major underground newspapers, came the following wordy denunciation by its coordinator, Tom Forcade:

> Underground is a sloppy word and a lot
> of us are sorry we got stuck with it.
> 'Underground' is meaningless, ambiguous,
> irrelevant, wildly imprecise, undefinitive,
> derivative, uncopyrighted, uncontrollable,
> and used up. . . .[3]

What then is meant by the unsatisfactory term, "underground press"? A 1967 *Esquire* magazine article by Michael Lyndon, entitled, "The Word Gets Out," explained, "The word creates a romantic spell and, with it, the papers and the revolution they herald become as great as the believer's power of imagination."[4] The phrase, then, is largely figurative and can be interpreted according to each reader's "power of imagination."

The larger question of which anti-establishment papers are more underground and which are less underground is not easily answered. The elusive character of the new medium reflects the continuously changing and varied interests of its audience. The underground press is a wildly unpredictable happening; constantly changing and mercurially fluid, it reflects and comments on an era faster moving than any other in history. Against this amorphous background the reader must understand that this book is merely an attempt to stop the camera for a moment in 1970 to check the film on approximately fifteen years of underground publishing.

One way to understand any underground paper is to determine which ground the publication's audience is under. In the San Francisco Bay Area, for instance, the editorial content of the Berkeley *Barb*, *The Ally*, and the *Movement* each are aimed at different underground audiences. One segment of the *Barb*'s audience identifies closely with anything opposed to the police or the courts. Thus *Barb* readers get columns of copy with headlines blaring, "Is Huey Newton's Judge A Racist?" or "Pigs On U.C. Campus!" *The Ally*, on the other hand, caters to a military audience and makes its biggest editorial pitch against the war in Vietnam and the Army brass; it circulates some 12,000 copies each month to readers who are under the ground of the brass and the war in Vietnam. A third Bay Area underground paper, the *Movement*, aims at a politically radical audience and thus runs news, pictures and even reviews of rock music groups with an emphasis on radical ideology.

Another way to look at the seemingly shapeless underground press is to analyze its audience. According to overground *Fortune* magazine the underground audience includes, "Hippies and doctrinnaire Leninists, anarchists and populists, the 'campus cong' and peaceful communards, militant confrontationists and mystics, Bakuninists and humanists, power seekers, ego trippers, revolutionaries, Maoists, rock bands, and cultural guerillas."[5]

Newspaper audiences in general want to read things from their own point of view. That is why there is William Buckley's *National Review* on the right and Gilbert A. Harrison's *The New Republic* on the left. Telling it like it is to third world students and minority and youthful readers means telling it the way they want to hear it. Thus in the underground press, cops are not "police officers" but "pigs;" the Governor of the State of California is not "the Governor" but "Rat Fink Reagan;" and all members of the Establishment in positions of authority are not "Director," "President," or "Chairman," but "the MAN." The very words the underground editors choose express the way they view, and want to view, society.

Large and small city dailies are almost always owned by the economic upper class, distributed to the middle class, and relatively unconcerned with the lower and alienated classes in American society. Consequently, underground editors declare that the traditional media always view crime stories from the side of the police. They say further that third world students and minority groups make the regular news columns mostly when the news about them is disparaging, such as in reports concerning racial riots, student unrest, or striking grape workers. A glance at the overground press any day of the week seems to bear them out.

Interviews with staffers, street sales people and the publishers of Philadelphia's *Distant Drummer*, New York City's *East Village Other*, Los Angeles' *Free Press*, Berkeley's *Barb*, the Washington, D.C., *Hard Times*, Detroit's *Fifth Estate* or Chicago's highly successful *Seed* indicate they are all under one ground or another.

Of the approximately 457 underground papers listed in the back of this book, 30 of the more prominent publications are here examined in depth. Attitudes toward oriental religion, drugs and the draft, the cops, rock music, flicks and confrontation politics are explored to pinpoint which underground papers are under which ground.

By traditional journalistic standards, much of the writing in the underground press is lurid, subjective and sometimes undecipherable. A more sympathetic description of their writing would be poetic, personal, frank, free-form and, above all, creative. Since most underground editors assume the traditional media incapable of telling the truth about anything important, they reason, "What's the point of objectivity?" It is perhaps its total distrust of American institutions that frees the underground press to attack anything and everything related to the American establishment.

For the business establishment, possibly the most surprising aspects of this study will be those dealing with the business and financial procedures employed by the majority of underground publishers. As the former publisher of a financially sound overground weekly newspaper, the author found most underground publishers both ignorant about and unconcerned with normal methods of accounting, advertising, distribution and organization. This statement is not intended as a one-sided criticism of the underground editors; indifference to economics is part of the underground movement's philosophy and its editors have intentionally refused to be tied up in the establishment's strait-jacket of debits, credits, and profit and loss statements. As might be expected, however, the more enduring underground papers learn and employ standard overground newspaper procedures in all areas except editorial and advertising content.

Another distinguishing characteristic of underground newspapers is that nearly all of their staffers earn their living from other sources. The objectives of the underground press are almost never related to profits, althought some of them operate at some profit. Most of the staffers work for the satisfaction of providing the opposition to what they consider a corrupt, materialistic American system.

There are approximately 1,752 dailies and 9,000 weeklies listed in the 1968 *Ayers' Directory of American Newspapers* and *Periodicals*. These are clearly not underground. The content and format of newspapers analyzed in the following pages is unlike that of traditional newspapers in almost all respects aside from their being tabloids printed with ink on paper. The underground press is concerned with what's *in* or current in confrontation politics, drugs, astrology, and race relations. Unlike the *New York Times*, most undergrounders would like to print all the news that's *unfit* to print.

No underground newspapers publish daily editions. Some of the more successful papers publish weekly, but most publish monthly, bi-monthly, or as one overworked editor of the understaffed *Black Panther* put it, "It's a weekly, man, but it's just that some weeks are longer than others."

Tom Hayden, one of the founders of Students for a Democratic Society (SDS) tells his followers that "action creates its own evidence." Evidence of the action of the underground press today is being found more and more in the reaction of the overground media. The underground newspapers, said one overground magazine article on student activists, "have attracted some excellent young writers and editors." And as the establishment becomes more aware of this talent they will almost certainly try to get a piece of the action and turn it into profits. In one such case the former managing editor of the Berkeley *Barb* quit his job, cut his shoulder-length hair and joined *Time*, the weekly newsmagazine, as a stringer. Traditional media have not yet figured out how to cash in on most of the works of these artists, reporters, and editors but you can be sure they are on to the possibilities of profit from this new source of talent.

SDS's Hayden recognizes the danger of the traditional media co-opting the major elements of the radical movement and clearly opposes all facets of the monied establishment. Before he would begin a University of California lecture series entitled "The New American Revolution," he ordered CBS, ABC, and Westinghouse television crews, who were in the classroom to film documentary material for commercial programming, to detach their cameras. Nonetheless the establishment is slowly but steadily findings ways to exploit the radical movement. For instance, notice television commercials pleading for the viewer to "Join the Dodge REBELLION!" or observe the implications of the Smothers' Brothers show that had Bob Newhart joking about getting stoned.

The established record companies are perhaps the closest and most visible collaborators with the new themes and language of the underground. Rock singer Grace Slick saying "fuck" on the respectable Columbia label or a rock band giving out with a loud, collective "bullshit" on an RCA album are further evidence of the establishment's determination to make profits from the underground prophets. Book publishers want in on the action, too. One Doubleday book editor said his company had offered fugitive Eldridge Cleaver, the former editor of the underground's militant *Black Panther*, $50,000 'for the publishing rights to his next two books. The same company has run display advertising on one book for the underground audience in the more prominent underground newspapers. The record companies also advertise heavily in the underground press.

Radio commercials and newspaper advertisements are just as eager to cash in on the underground movement. Many college students are reading ads like the one from AT&T seeking college graduates with underground oracle Bob Dylan's message, "The Times They Are A-Changin'," in 84-point type in the headline. And radio commercials for cigarettes, shoes, and clothes are increasingly using the turned-on music and language of the underground's drug set.

Action not only creates its own evidence but it also breeds reaction, and the action of the underground press is breeding a possibly destructive reaction from the established authorities and from traditional media. No doubt, the establishment can learn plenty from the youth movement, the radicals, and their utterances in the underground press. The danger to the underground is, however, that if the profit-minded establishment buys in, will that mean that the underground press will be watered down, co-opted, and forced to sell out? The possibilities for the underground and subsequent threat to the overground is that they may continue to infiltrate the establishment and their media and turn them on to the underground's radical view of American society. The chapter on "Influencing the Overground" speaks to these and related questions and will touch on the effect the underground press has on clothes, hair, music, education, sex, and political behavior in the overground establishment.

In talking with many journalism educators before deciding to write this book, the author found a scoffing disregard and a corresponding ignorance of the scope or dimension of the underground press in America. Most educators take the view, "If we're quiet maybe they'll go away and we won't have to deal with them." Consequently, most educators are shocked to learn that in Berkeley, California, the *Barb* has, on any publication Thursday, nearly six times the circulation (85,000) of the conservative, establishment *Berkeley Gazette* (14,299).

The underground press in America is not going to go away and it is not going to disappear. Its total circulation presently approaches five million, competing with the influential college press in America. Thus, the sooner journalism educators, establishment publishers, and the public in general realize the scope, impact, and influence of the underground press in America, the sooner they will give it the attention it deserves and understand it as the journalistic and social phenomenon that it is.

2 / Historical Perspective

A Modern View

*We're simply chronicling the progress
of the atomic children. We're for the
young and the eternally young. The
people open to change.*

—WALTER BOWART
East Village Other[1]

THE KEY POLITICAL, SOCIAL, AND TECHNICAL DEVELOP-
ments that prepared the way for the underground press in themselves give almost enough material for a cultural history of the
youth movement in America. The social and political indifference
of the Eisenhower years, the youthful involvement in the Southern
civil rights movement, the drug culture of the early 60s, the moral
resentment of the war in Vietnam, and the bitterness toward a
government incapable of solving racial and poverty problems in the
world's wealthiest nation—this is only a rough sketch of the background from which the underground press began to emerge.

The history of the underground press in America is largely a
chronicle of youthful reaction to the technical, political, and cultural conditions in the American society. Following the development of underground publications over the past fifteen years is
much like following the development of a gifted and frustrated
child during that disturbing and chaotic decade and a half. The

era offered the advantage of unprecedented economic and technological growth, but coupled with that was the frustration of static social and political institutions. Thanks to the growth, the awakening child had the leisure to contemplate the dilemma of a twentieth century technology strapped with seventeenth century institutions. His contemplation found expression in the new journalism.

The underground press in America, as does all new media, threatened its established predecessors. The fledgling press was attacked, harassed, and rejected by the established press in phrases like the "outlaw press," the "outhouse press," and the "seedier media." An obvious and not insignificant reason for the development of the underground in modern America was that the overground press did not speak to the problems of a widening new subculture, a subculture that had become more educated and thus was more in need of its own communication medium. Rebuffed, rejected, and soon alienated, the underground press found a ready audience among the subcultures of American society. Street people and hippies, drug addicts and poor whites joined with college students, black militants, poets and intellectuals to create a new coalition of readers for the alternative medium.

This subculture had begun its unsteady coalescence in the beatnik heyday of Bohemian young men and ultimately burst forth to include the children of American affluence. Men like Jack Kerouac, Allan Ginsberg, Aldous Huxley, Paul Goodman, Lenny Bruce, Marshall McLuhan and William Burroughs were in the forefront providing the words while Bob Dylan, the Beatles, and the Grateful Dead poured forth much of the poetry and music. While these artists, poets and prophets painted a picture of social injustice, cultural inequity and racial oppression, men like Norman Mailer, Paul Krassner, Art Kunkin, John Bryan, Max Scheer, Allan Katzman, Walter Bowart and John Wilcock sat at their Justiwriters and created a whole new phenomenon, a fifth estate in American journalism.

The first underground publications in modern day America were the *Village Voice* and the *Realist*, both started in New York City. They were largely a response to the social indifference and journalistic vacuum at the end of the silent generation of the 1950s. The radical *Guardian* was founded in 1948, well before the *Voice* or the *Realist*, but was, at that time, considered a political organ and thus a special interest publication, not much different from a union house organ. The *Guardian* is now very much underground; extremely well written, it is probably the finest nationally-distributed, radically-political paper.

The first *Village Voice* was produced in New York City's Greenwich Village on October 26, 1955. The *Voice* was, in one sense, a reaction to an inane Village publication called, unimaginatively enough, *The Villager*. *The Villager* was, says Jerry Tollmer, *New York Post* drama critic and one of the *Voice* founders, "published for little old ladies with cats." According to Tollmer, New York's Greenwich Village was then run by a cabal of Tammany Hall Democrats, Republicans, and Mafia types reported on by *The Villager*, which never bothered to cover the more exciting Village Independent Democrats. Norman Mailer, Edwin Fancher, Daniel Wolf, and John Wilcock, the other *Voice* founders, simply covered the VID meetings and found an instant audience hungry for liberally-slanted political and cultural news of the Village. The *Voice* was not only a reaction to the *Villager* but also to the New York dailies' lack of coverage of what was the beginning of the Beat or Hip generation of the Village.

Before the *Voice*, artists, poets, critics, writers, pseudo-writers, and all kinds of hangers-on and social drop-outs frequented the Village's Bohemian pubs, park benches, and book stores without any published voice in the Village. Fancher, Mailer, and Wolf were perhaps the fathers of today's "Do-Your-Own-Thing" generation since they started the *Village Voice*, according to Fancher, "because we wanted to publish a newspaper the way we wanted to."

That the *Village Voice* of 1970 is not nearly so underground as New York City's *East Village Other*, the *Rat* (a newspaper of "subterranean news"), or the *Guardian* does not diminish its pioneering position in the history of the underground press. And if it is now only partially underground it nonetheless includes as wide a variety of coverage and contributors as any other American weekly newspaper—over- or underground.

Tom Forcade of the Underground Press Syndicate has observed, "The more underground a publication the more radically it is opposed to the society in which it operates." Most underground editors, particularly the political radicals, find the Voice timid, if not downright traitorous to their cause. A unique characteristic of the underground press is that it considers the sharing of material a fundamental part of press freedom. Fancher claims that his publication does all its own reporting and argues that other papers should do the same. The policy is considered conservative and greedy by underground editors and is the main reason for the Voice's disfavor among underground editorial leaders and radical movement people in general.

The Voice was also the first newspaper in the history of modern American journalism to consistently report news with no restriction on language, a policy widely adopted by underground editors to shock the authority structure. The Voice was also the first paper to give unsung and unpublished authors from the Village's substantial bank of creative talent a chance to be heard. Over the years, the Voice's list of contributors is a Who's Who in topical American journalism. Just a handful of those contributors to the Voice were Michael Harrington, Norman Mailer, William Burroughs, Nat Hentoff, Katherine Anne Porter, Allan Ginsberg, Joseph Lyford, Anais Nin, Jack Newfield, Vance Bourjaily, and Donald Carpenter.

John Wilcock, an original Voice staff member and a ubiquitous figure in the development of the underground press in America, believes that all good editors should be troublemakers. If Don Wolf provided the idea for the Voice and Ed Fancher the drive for economic stability, Mailer most certainly provided the trouble. Although Mailer still owned fifteen per cent of the Voice stock in 1969, he wrote for the paper only through its first eighteen issues. About those tumultuous beginning issues Mailer later admitted, "At heart, I wanted a war." In one sense it can be said that Mailer was one of the few visionaries of underground publishing. Mailer could see the revolution on the horizon, but his partners wanted to make a financial success of the paper and well they did. After the *Voice* lost nearly $1,000 a week during the first year, a disgusted Mailer had thrown in his hand. He later wrote, "They wanted it to be successful, I wanted it to be outrageous. I had the feeling of an underground revolution on its way, and I do not know that I was wrong."[2] Mailer was right, but as *Playboy* magazine reported, "It was, as ever, the sad destiny of his [Mailer's] intelligence to be ready for revolution before the troops were ready."[3] Of course, Mailer did not drop from the scene and his reporting of the national political conventions, *Miami and the Siege of Chicago*, was a vivid and astonishing portrayal of the chaotic American democratic process, as well as a substantial contribution to the "new journalism."

The troops weren't yet ready and the few "bridge" publications in the late 50s and early 60s were basically only temporary, independent journals of dissent. Although no important publications emerged to oppose the Establishment, the transition papers fluttered for awhile, barely left the ground, then died. One such publication was a New York weekly called *East* which claimed a circulation of 27,000, although its circulation manager at the time has estimated that the readers numbered closer to 2,700. It died after a few years. *Beatitude* lasted less than a year in San Francisco while other short-lived, irregularly-published mimeographed sheets began to spread the anti-establishment word. *Aardvark* and *Big Table* fizzled in Chicago while the West Coast continued to produce such exhibitionistic, scatological journals as the *Idiot* and *Horseshit*, the latter published by Southern California's Scum Press. Bert Wolf's *Californian* and North Beach's *San Francisco Star* lasted a year or two, then folded.

Hundreds of mimeographed publications have sprung up over the past twenty years to defend fetishism, fags, teeny boppers, scatology, sex, and radical politics. The historical point is that most of them fizzled after a few harried issues or months while only the Voice and the Realist persisted until the youthful revolution arrived.

Whatever the Voice is or is not in the eyes of its underground counterparts, it is still the largest circulated weekly newspaper, 130,000 ABC (Audit Bureau of Circulation), in the United States, under- or overground, and has a larger circulation than 93 per cent of America's dailies. The Voice's increase in circulation largely parallels the increase in all underground papers over the last six years. By 1965 the Voice had a circulation of 27,796 according to ABC. By late 1969 the Voice was up to 130,000, an increase of over 100,000 paid readers. The only notable underground papers in 1965 were the Berkeley Barb, the East Village Other, and the Los Angeles Free Press whose total circulation was less than 50,000. By 1969, however, they had a collective circulation in excess of 200,000.

If the Village Voice broke the four-letter word barrier, the Realist, started by Paul Krassner in 1958, broke almost every other barrier. Krassner, at the time a 26-year-old contributor to Mad Magazine, began publishing what came to be considered "the magazine of irreverence" in an era when most American institutions were considered above and beyond ridicule by traditional media. Krassner claimed, "Reverence must be earned. A person or an institution does not deserve respect or reverence simply because he is President or because it is powerful." In the first issues, the witty and colorful Krassner kept changing the subtitle on the masthead, from "The Magazine of Irreverence," to "The Magazine of Cherry Pie and Violence," to the "Magazine of Wrongeous Indignation," to the "Magazine of Applied Paranoia," or to anything that would shock or startle his readers out of any sanctimonious seriousness.

Krassner explained the instant sucess of his publication when he said, "All of those crazy Mad Magazine readers had grown up and needed a more mature publication." Krassner gave them what they wanted by attacking every sacred cow on the American horizon. "God is Alive in Argentina" or "The Sex Life of J. Edgar Hoover" were timid topics for Krassner who found no subject too hot to handle. Krassner explained, "A newspaper is supposed to report the news, not perpetuate the status quo." The *Realist* did something other than report the news as it ran shocking but often humorous features entitled, "Computer Calculated Copulation," "I was an Abortionist for the FBI" or "A Kick in the Inaugural Balls." In a statement on policy headlined "Where the Realist Is At" Krassner quipped, "I'm not paranoid enough to believe that harassment is any sort of conspiracy against me, although someone high up did warn: 'You're on the government's shit list, you know!' That's a coincidence, I replied. The government's on my shit list."[4] Someone must have wanted to read the *Realist's* bizarre view of American society because in ten years its circulation grew from 600 to 150,000 and Krassner expected his Tenth Anniversary Issue (thirteen months late in 1969) to reach 200,000 readers.

The *Village Voice* taught the new breed of journalists two things. First it proved that the Bohemian contributors from New York's Greenwich Village could find a home within the newspaper format. Artists, beatniks, poets, critics, and drifters were all included in the new formula provided by Wolf, Mailer, and Fancher. The second lesson was that a newspaper could be different and survive. Traditional journalism in America was notoriously close to being merely a medium for advertisers selling commodities. The *Voice*, if not the *Realist*, gave wings to the failing dream that American journalism could be dedicated to informing *all* segments of the American electorate.

The next historically significant underground publication confirmed those two lessons. The Los Angeles *Free Press* was started in May 1964 and was modeled after the *Village Voice*. Art Kunkin, a 37-year-old critic of the American dream started the *Freep*, as it is called by its hip readers, with virtually no editorial or publishing experience. The first issue of *Freep* was distributed free at the Renaissance Fayre sponsored by radio station KPFK and was first called the *Faire Free Press*. The *Freep* soon gained the reputation of being *against* police brutality and President Lyndon Johnson's Great Society and *for* acid heads, rock music, and classified mating-game sex advertisements. The classified ads which were mostly "for girls to share housekeeping with lonely studs" have been quoted widely in writing on the underground press and aptly reflect a segment of the diverse, casual, permissive Southern California life style.

Once again the underground press was a reaction, this time to an uptight and unconcerned Southern California journalism scene where the leading newspaper, the *Los Angeles Times* admitted having no contact with the subculture of Watts, the rock music world, or the unpredictably explosive cult of motorcyclists. In six years the *Freep*, which had started in a garage with $15 capital, grew from a four-page, small circulation giveaway, to a forty-eight page weekly of 95,000 paid circulation with expenditures of over $15,000 per issue.

Other publications have flourished temporarily in Los Angeles but only *Freep* has persisted.

Most notable among those now-defunct papers were the Los Angeles *Oracle* and John Bryan's *Open City*. The *Oracle* was almost totally dedicated to drug users and their psychedelic lore and rose to 60,000 circulation before their founders, Joe Dana and Victor Pawlock, called it quits in 1967.

John Bryan's *Open City* has a more interesting and significant history. Started in San Francisco in November 1964 as the *San Francisco Open City Press*, Bryan's virgin publishing effort lasted but four issues in the Bay Area. A former music critic and reporter for both the *San Francisco Examiner* and *Chronicle*, Bryan launched his anti-establishment sheet with a $700 severance check from the *Chronicle* plus a multigraph printing press picked up cheaply as a U.S. Army reject. After the San Francisco effort folded Bryan took a job as Sunday Magazine editor for William Randolph Hearst's *Herald-Examiner* in Los Angeles, where he lasted less than two years. When told by his superiors that a woodcut of the

Madonna and Christ Child was unacceptable because the Christ Child's penis was showing, Bryan quit in a huff and joined Kunkin's *Free Press* as managing editor. In his first article for the *Freep*, about the rejection of the Christ Child woodcut, he referred to the *Herald-Examiner*'s "Castrating Christ for Christmas."

Growth in circulation and advertising came to the *Freep* and along with it the inevitable need for business organization and staff control. When the U.S. Labor Department forced Kunkin to install time clocks for his staff, Bryan was infuriated by such constriction and left to start *Open City* in May 1967. *Open City* lasted less than two years but not before it had experimented with some highly unusual free form graphics within the broadside format. *Open City* was the only significant underground publication to use this format, although Boston's *Avatar* tried it for a few issues before returning to tabloid and, in August 1969, San Francisco's *Dock of the Bay* started its publication in broadside. While it operated, *Open City* became the underground newspaper voice of rock music. When it folded, *Rolling Stone* and *Distant Drummer* had replaced it in that category, with the bimonthly *Rolling Stone* reaching a circulation of 300,000 by June 1970. Like rock, *Open City* became personal, hypertense, colorful, and totally uninhibited. Bryan had a penchant for all aspects of sexual freedom but law suits and court costs ultimately forced him out of business in March 1969. Scatologically typical was an issue that included articles on "Jail Rapes," "The Playboy Tease," "Astro-Masturbation," "Art To Screw By," plus a photograph of a young woman carrying a sign "Every Woman Secretly Wants To Be Raped."[5] Bryan's obsession with sex is indicated by the fact that when he left *Open City* he moved back to San Francisco where he claimed he was "writing pornographic novels with plans to start a West Coast version of the *New York Review of Sex*." Bryan's seemingly imbalanced emphasis on sexual freedom should not detract from the very real contributions he made to psychedelic art, free form layout, and reporting of the rock and *freaky* cultural scene in Los Angeles.

Two other publications that must be mentioned in a history of development of the underground press in America are: the Berkeley *Barb*, a reaction to a staid Berkeley press and a monolithic university administration, and New York City's *East Village Other*, a reaction to what had become a more conservative *Village Voice*.

The *Barb* is a mystery to most students of American journalism as well as to many undeground editors themselves. Often referred to as the world's ugliest newspaper, the *Barb* in three years became one of the underground's most successful publications in circulation and financial stability. The secret of the *Barb's* success had clearly been Max Scherr, a lifelong radical in his middle fifties who looks very much like the radical youngsters and street people his paper serves. An avid troublemaker, Scherr produced the *Barb* out of his old, rambling Berkeley home where his wife initially cooked all the meals for his staff. In June 1969 Scherr's staff came upon information from a satirical sheet, *The Berkeley Fascist*, suggesting Scherr had been netting a profit of $5,000 a week from their efforts. After a strike and considerable legal maneuvering, twenty members of the staff, calling themselves the Red Mountain Tribe (after an inexpensive California red wine) formed their own organization and started the Berkeley *Tribe*. Depressed over the loss of what he called "my children," Scherr sold the *Barb* to Allan Coult, a Timothy Leary generation cultural revolutionary. Coult operated the *Barb* for a few stormy months until December 15, 1969, at which time the court awarded the paper back to Scherr pending final settlement, since Coult had allegedly reneged on payments to Scherr. The *Tribe* persuaded former *Barb* editor Jim Schreiber to return to underground newspapering (he was a stringer for *Time* and *Newsweek* at the time) and the first *Tribe* issues denounced Scherr as "a corrupt prophet and a greedy fascist pig." Scherr had sold the *Barb* to Coult for an estimated $200,000 and Coult's third issue announced the following ambitious objectives:

1. *End the war in Vietnam. Stop the draft. Empty the military stockades.*

2. *Turn the military-industrial-educational complex to peaceful uses.*

3. Destroy the power of universities
and colleges by establishing real centers of learning in
order to expand consciousness and to foster Zen and Yoga
and meaningful use of psychedelic drugs.

4. Support complete sexual freedom between consenting
individuals, and provide true knowledge of the sexual nature
of man.

5. Help all oppressed people.

6. Free people of greed, hate and corruption.

7. Free children from all oppression—at home, at school, and
elsewhere—so that the next generation will be healthy,
sexual, and enlightened.

8. Support complete freedom of all media.

9. Support the repeal of abortion laws.

10. Work to provide meaningful vocations where people can
use their creative talents.

11. End unfair taxation, and the taxation that favors the rich.

12. Free the country from governmental parasitism.

13. End hypocrisy.
Love not hate.   Hate not Love.[6]

But back to the original *Barb*. Founded on Friday, August 13,
1965, Scherr funded the first *Barb* issues with money received from
the sale of his Steppenwolf bar in Berkeley. The paper grew largely
because of Scherr's insistence on putting out a paper for the street
people and not for the liberal left elite. Berkeley is a university city
and Scherr's dislike for the university administration won the
hearts and readership of the alienated members of the Bay Area's
youth and student movement. Scherr said, "I am not seeking the
understanding of my readers. I want my readers to feel it." Feel it
they did as his garish use of black ink and slapdash layouts represented exactly what the turned-on, dropped-out Berkeley subculture wanted. In one sense the *Barb* defied all the sound principles
of newspaper make-up, art, and design. The end product, however,
was exciting and very much in tune with where Berkeley was at
in the middle and late 1960s. But the rigors of underground pub-

lishing had their price. By April 1970, Coult had died suddenly and the saddened Scherr was in hospital with a heart attack.

Another newspaper that does much to capture the spirit of underground publishing is New York's *East Village Other*. Started in October 1965 by poet Allan Katzman, painter Walter Bowart, and the ubiquitous journalist John Wilcock, *EVO* was called "the Bat Masterson" of the underground press. Katzman, the only founder still with *EVO* in 1969, claims that it was the first publication in America to think of a newspaper as an art form. The innovative concept of presenting news without columns, comics as editorial comment, and color as a vehicle of emotional expression were first introduced to the underground press by *EVO*. Bowart was an artist intent on trying new and different ways of expressing his view of reality within the newspaper format. The first *EVO*s ran headlines and stories sideways, in circles, off the page, or any way Bowart and Katzman thought would break old newspaper patterns. In one sense it can be said that *EVO* introduced art to the news columns of the medium although it was a later publication, the *San Francisco Oracle*, that pushed the concept to new limits.

In November of that year in Detroit, Harvey Ovshinsky, a 19-year-old dropout from the Los Angeles *Free Press*, started the *Fifth Estate* in Detroit. *Fifth Estate* relies heavily on news packets from the Liberation News Service and fillers from the Underground Press Syndicate, two centralized organizations servicing the underground. This paper is important historically because there were so few publishing at the time, but runs little in-depth or live news in its columns. Jacob Brackman in a *Playboy* magazine article said the *Fifth Estate* "isn't much more than a hick cut and paste job of pilfered material." Although *Fifth Estate* has always been politically radical, it is considered quite ordinary by underground editors. Ovshinsky explained how he named the paper in his first issue:

> There are four estates, the fourth of which is journalism. We are the fifth because we are something different than . . . other newspapers. We hope to fill a void in that fourth estate.

... A void created by party newspapers and the cutting of those articles which might express the more liberal viewpoint. That's what we really are—the voice of the liberal element . . . We want to be a truly free press. We will be labeled radical, socialist and communist. But you can call us just 'honest.' It's what we're going to try hard to be.[7]

Ovshinsky left the paper in 1969 to do hospital work in the Detroit area and the new directors' plans were to emphasize music, theater, and live reporting more than their predecessor.

The next paper to develop, the *San Francisco Oracle*, is probably the major exception to the rule of reaction among papers of the new cultural and political left. In the summer of 1966 a political group representing the Progressive Labor Party put out one issue which they called *P. O. Frisco*. "P. O." stood for Psychedelic Oracle but the issue was, as expected, light on psychedelics and heavy on politics. The reaction from the Haight-Ashbury community was unenthusiastic and the *Oracle* directors learned that radical politics was not to be an important part of their format.

Started September 20, 1966, by a group of artists, poets, journalists, and Haight-Ashbury flower children, the *San Francisco Oracle* generally copied other underground papers through the first three issues. The two original editors, George Tsongas and John Brownson, made the first *Oracles* look rather ordinary. When they departed, a more creative group took over. During the next nine issues the *San Francisco Oracle* was probably the most exciting, (Plate 1) graphically experimental newspaper in America. It was written and designed at Rod and Jay Thelin's Psychedelic Shop in the "Haight" where Gabe Katz, Steve Levine, and Allen Cohen put together some of the most unusual art, poetry, prophesy, and graphics ever assembled within the newspaper format. The first issues of the *Oracle* brought together some of the older members of the hip community along with the newer spokesmen of the emerging San Francisco renaissance. Those issues included materials from Buckminster Fuller, Robert Theobald, Allan Ginsberg, Ken Kesey, Bob Kaufman, John Sinclair, Norman Mailer,

Allan Watts, Gary Snyder, Timothy Leary, Chet Helms, Rick Griffin, Michael McClure, and Jerry Rubin. The first issue contained a satire on the Declaration of Independence which proclaimed "freedom of the body, the pursuit of joy and the expansion of consciousness"[8] as inalienable American rights. The art work was as creative as anything that has since been tried in the underground press and the writing was at once religious, defiant, demanding, and literate. The first use of split fountain rainbow colors bleeding into one another turned on the underground readers to say nothing of the jaw-dropping effect it had on conventional newspaper observers.

In one sense it can be said that the San Francisco Oracle reflected the colorful, psychedelic life style that surrounded "The Haight." More significant, however, was the whole new marriage of a colorful community to a newspaper which set the standards of graphic excellence for all underground papers to follow. After twelve issues were produced over a seventeen-month period, the San Francisco Oracle, as it represented that brief "flower child era," ceased publication. Its directors Cohen, Levine, and Katz believed "The Haight" was no longer a place that would support creativity in the Oracle format. Other more commercially oriented people picked up the Oracle masthead but it never measured up to the standards of its originators.

The other significant underground birth of 1966 was the Washington Free Press. It was founded by Michael Grossman and Arthur Grosman, both students at the Washington, D.C., Institute of Policy Studies along with Margie Stamberg, later with the Guardian, Sheila Ryan, later with Liberation News Service, Bill Blum, and Frank Speltz. The Free Press was more concerned with federal government activities than was any other underground paper but by 1969 it was emphasizing radical politics and scatology. (Plate 2) While the Washington Free Press once had a children's page with poetry and beautiful illustrations, by the summer of 1969 Tato, the Mexican-imported revolutionary editor, preferred columns entitled "Fuck the System" and other politically radical material programmed to infuriate the Washington establishment. By mid-1969 the editors had been so successful at angering the local authorities (six arrests in two days) with their attacks on narcotics agents and judges (one issue pictured a local magistrate masturbating into a computer with a caption reading "He' Comm D' Judge") that it appeared future issues would have to be printed in upstate New York or out of the country entirely.

The next rash of underground newspaper births came as a reaction to the unpopular and frustrating Vietnam war. In New York Ed Sanders, who published the outrageous *Fuck You/A Magazine of the Arts*, wrote a position paper that stated:

> It makes us puke green monkey shit to contemplate Johnson's war in Viet Nam. Lyndon Baines is squirting the best blood of America into a creep scene. Kids are 'gook bricking' in Asia without thought, without reason, without law.[9]

This kind of intense reaction to a war that an increasing number of Americans believed was a tactical as well as a moral blunder brought a whole new breed of papers into the underground movement. In May 1967, Earl "The Mole" Segal produced a radical paper called the *Seed* from a north side Chicago head shop called, after its owner, "The Mole Hole." In June Mel Lyman followed with the graphically delightful Boston *Avatar*. The next month two graduate students in Stanford, California, started a well-written, anti-Stanford, anti-Palo Alto city government publication called the *Mid-Peninsula Observer*. Before the year of the Vietnam summer demonstrations was over, John Kois, a *Milwaukee Journal* drop-out, had started *Kaleidoscope* in Milwaukee, and Don De Maio, a frustrated *Wall Street Journal* staffer had founded *Distant Drummer* in conservative Philadelphia.

Before any of those publications began printing in 1967, the *Black Panther* produced its first paper on April 27 as a reaction to a completely different kind of injustice—racial inequality. The *Black Panther* was founded by Huey Newton and Bobby Seale in Oakland, California. This newspaper is the main organ for the

Black Panther Party in America and is dedicated to gaining equality for black or oppressed people the world over. In the June 7, 1969, issue was published the following ten-point program outlining the purpose of the party and the paper:

1. *We want freedom. We want power to determine the destiny of our Black Community.*
2. *We want full employment for our people.*
3. *We want an end to the robbery by the white man of our Black Community.*
4. *We want decent housing, fit for shelter of human beings.*
5. *We want education for our people that exposes the true nature of this decadent American society. We want education that teaches us our true history and our role in the present-day society.*
6. *We want all black men to be exempt from military service.*
7. *We want an immediate end to* POLICE BRUTALITY *and* MURDER *of Black people.*
8. *We want freedom for all black men held in federal, state, county and city prisons and jails.*
9. *We want all black people when brought to trial to be tried in court by a jury of their peer group or people from their black communities, as defined by the Constitution of the United States.*
10. *We want land, bread, housing, education, clothing, justice and peace. And as our major political objective, a United Nations-supervised plebiscite to be held throughout the black colony in which only black colonial subjects will be allowed to participate, for the purpose of determining the will of black people as to their national destiny.*[10]

With a national circulation of approximately 85,000 the *Black Panther* works closely with movement people on other underground papers; in the summer of 1969 it housed the typesetting equipment for at least three other Bay Area publications. The *Black Panther* is a 24-page tabloid weekly, uses color effectively and directs all its editorial firepower toward helping black and third world people fight oppression. Malcolm X, Huey Newton and Eldridge Cleaver are the paper's heroes while any racist member of white America or "The MAN" (a term symbolizing any person or organization that has authority over them) are their enemies. Contrary to much bad publicity in the white-dominated establishment press, the Panther organization conducts many positive and helpful projects in the black community. Their Free Breakfast Program is a model of self-help for peoples everywhere and their education program in black ghettoes is both personal and effective compared to many government-sponsored poverty programs.

Chicago's colorful, psychedelic *Seed* is a study in the flexibility and versatility of underground staff members. Not only were there no founders on the staff in 1969, but none of the staffers had been there over twelve months. *Seed* business manager Terry Sibela explained "after one year in this bat cage, it gets to be like a bummer marriage." Abe Peck, the editor for nearly a year had reportedly just left for Alaska in June 1969 and staff writer Mike Abrahamson had taken over. *Seed* has a lighter touch than most underground papers and regularly urges its readers to "get stoned a lot, laugh, dance and meditate." Liberal with color and expensive newspaper stock, *Seed* runs light-hearted and irreverent fillers to offset the heavy tone in competing, politically based underground papers. Around a beautiful halftone center spread of mountains and lakes, a June 1969 issue printed the following items:

> *Tuli Kupferberg of the Fugs used to mail*
> *his snot to the power company in New York.*

or

> *Construct a giant toothbrush and drag*
> *it along the beach. Chicago has bad breath.*

or

> *Run naked thru the streets with a sign*
> *saying "Eat Me" hanging from your*

> *derriere. If someone offers, tell*
> *he or she that you'd like to oblige*
> *but that, alas, your DDT level of*
> *12 parts/million makes you a hazard.*[11]

The *Seed* prints 24,000 papers at a multiple publishing plant in Wisconsin and does all its own camera work, delivering negatives to the printer ready for plate making. Most undergrounders don't have a copy camera but Miss Sebela claimed that theirs saved them $5,000 a year in production costs. The talented Miss Sebela can run all of the typesetting and camera equipment and fills in on paste up, bookkeeping, and reporting when needed. Two or three of the other staffers do the same when the printer's deadline nears. *Seed* is located in a deserted Chicago bar ironically called "The Bohemian Club" and staffers refer to the production department as "the bat cave of the underground." Although *Seed* is imaginatively presented, it publishes somewhat irregularly. "Irregularly" to the *Seed* usually means every two or three weeks, which is probably why Milwaukee's *Kaleidoscope* began to publish a weekly edition for Chicago in late 1969.

John Kois, Bob Deitman, and John Sahli founded *Kaleidoscope* in Milwaukee as an alternative to traditional midwestern newspapers in general and to the Milwaukee evening *Journal* and morning *Sentinel* in particular. *Kaleidoscope* started with 3,500 copies and one edition and had grown by late 1969 to 40,000 copies and editions in Milwaukee, Chicago, and Madison. Kois wanted *Kaleidoscope* to be "strictly a Midwestern thing," with the second section distributed as a free insert to underground papers in Indianapolis, Minneapolis, and any other Midwestern undergrounder requesting it.

Kaleidoscope is one of the most carefully-edited papers in the underground and includes a wide range of editorial content. The February 24–27, 1969, issue is typical in its diversity with stories on police harassment, high school turmoil, women's liberation news, drugs and how to get them, underground comics, pictures of nudes, and criticism of American society in general. *Kaleido-scope* always runs color and prepares its copy more carefully than most overground weeklies. For that reason it is one of the most respected papers in the Midwest among underground editors and readers.

Since most underground newspaper staffs resent authority or structure, the papers are usually run by editorial boards or co-ordinating committees. The *Avatar* in Boston, on the other hand, was the epitome of a paper that was the length and shadow of one man—Mel Lyman. He had led the Forte Hill communications center and commune where thirty young people lived, producing records, films, and, most notably, a slick, oversized magazine called *American Avatar*. *Avatar* became a newspaper in June 1967, starting in its new format as a sixteen-page, philosophical tabloid journal. In that issue, one column, "Who is the Underground?" ended with these lines:

> Who is the Underground?
> You are, if you think, dream, work, and build towards the
> improvements and changes in your life, your social and personal
> environments, towards the expectations of a better existence.
> Who is the Underground?
> The person next to you on the streetcar, as he proceeds to be
> where he wishes to be and do what he wishes to do.
> Who is the Underground?
> Think—look around—
> maybe in a mirror
> maybe inside. . . .[12]

Heavy on philosophical interpretation of current issues, the *Avatar* emphasized the occult and astrological aspects of the youth movement. While it published, the *Avatar* was graphically one of the most sophisticated of the underground newspapers with artistic use of green, soft blue, and orange inks on its cover and center pages.

Considered an ego tripper by most underground editors, Lyman announced in the first issue:

> To those of you unfamiliar with me let me introduce myself by saying that I am not a man, not a personality, not a tormented struggling individual. I am all those things but much much more, I am the truth and I speak the truth. I do not express ideas, opinions, personal views. I speak the truth. My understanding is tinged by no prejudice, no unconscious motivation, no confusion. I speak clearly, simply, openly and I speak only to reveal, to teach, to guide. I have no delusions about what I am, who I am, why I am. I have no pride to contend with, no hopes, no fears. In all humility I tell you I am the greatest man in the world and it doesn't trouble me in the least.[13]

Avatar ran a few issues in broadside format, a few tabloids on super white coated stock, and a few issues with yards of white space. When the Boston authorities came down on them for using four letter words, the publishers answered by publishing a center spread made up entirely of four letter words. Experimental, innovative, and highly creative, the *Avatar* did everything it wanted to do as a newspaper and then stopped publishing in March 1968. (Plate 3) In December, the *Avatar* began again, this time in the magazine format. An *Avatar* secretary explained the magazine's disdain for radical politics saying, "Life works in outward (or political) and inward (or spiritual) cycles. We are now in our spiritual cycle."

The *Avatar* has been an interesting testimony to the disinterest of most underground publishers in power or possession. Their willingness to die or to try a new medium of communication gives them a tremendous advantage over most traditional papers. It is difficult to imagine a traditional newspaper publisher saying, "The hell with our legal and national advertising contracts and income. Close the paper down and we'll start a magazine."

The next publication to emerge was the small but well written college-based *Peninsula Observer* in Palo Alto, California. Founded as a reaction to Stanford University's hammerlock on the local power structure, the *Observer* was staffed by students and educated observers of the Palo Alto scene. Not particularly radical or innovative by *Oracle* or *Realist* standards, the *Observer* did a steady job of investigative and analytical reporting in a twenty-page, bimonthly black and white format. The editors operated on a rotating basis and shared responsibilities for production, advertising, and distribution.

The *Observer* was started during the 1967 Vietnam summer and was instrumental in challenging the relevance and validity of ROTC on the Stanford campus. Many faculty and interested adults contributed financially to support the *Observer*, including a Palo Alto school board member who donated $25 checks on a regular basis. Sophisticated news topics such as air and water pollution, ecological and transportation problems were grist for the *Observer's* editorial mill. The *Observer* played down scatology and nude photography, since its suburban audience was more attuned to local politics and university matters.

The last of the historically significant underground papers that started in 1967 was Philadelphia's *Distant Drummer*. It was first issued in November as a response to what founder Don De Maio considered "a conservative and dishonest Philadelphia press." The *Distant Drummer* is an unusual underground paper because of its interest in economic security, which results in its steering away from involvement in radical politics. As a policy, the *Drummer* avoids obscene language, although it has, on occasion, used all the words, radical politics, and subjective reporting. The *Drummer's* favorite news topics are rock music (which brings in advertising lineage), local politics, book and theatre reviews, and cultural subjects in general. When asked the purpose of his publication, De Maio responded in about the same way an overground publisher would: "The purpose of the paper is to survive." This homage to the established money god makes the *Drummer* anathema to other undergrounders, particularly the competing SDS-associated *Philadelphia Free Press* which started a year later.

The moral outrage of the 1967 Vietnam summer turned to

radical political vision by 1968 as several new papers began. High school students found classrooms dead, teachers bored, the Vietnam war and the draft both intolerable and threatening. Since many high school and college administrators controlled and censored the school papers, radical students in America reacted with their own underground papers. In New York City the nationally established Liberation News Service (LNS) became the headquarters for the High School Independent Press Service (HIPS) and, by October 1968, HIPS had 400 paid subscribers from high school undergrounders across the country.

Little of the psychedelic art, sense of humor, or cosmic observations accompanied the politically new left publications. They swung heavily to confrontation politics, opposition to the draft and the military, the black liberation movement, labor problems, the struggles of working people, and the youthful revolt that was under way. The tempo of the political movement was increasing and the quality and preparation of new underground editors increased along with it. In January, Marvin Garson, a graduate in History from Berkeley's University of California, started the *San Francisco Express-Times* with some money from co-founder Bob Novick and funds from *Macbird*, a play satirizing President Johnson, written by his wife Barbara Garson.

Many people associated with the *San Francisco Express-Times* (later to become the *Good Times*) thought its editor, Marvin Garson, was a madman. Others thought him a genius, and still others thought him to be the only sane underground publisher in radical politics. Whatever Garson was or was not the *Good Times* was a change for Bay Area readers from the scatological, brash, and heavy-handed Berkeley *Barb*. By March 1968, Garson's paper was circulating 10,000 copies. Concerned with producing a publication "with class, not for the mass," Garson used tasteful layout and color combinations to achieve a near-slick magazine effect. In steady opposition to the *Barb* where he formerly worked, the explosive Garson quipped, "The *Barb's* like the *Reader's Digest*, we're like *Harper's*." If Garson was a moderate revolutionary before the 1968 Democratic Convention, his arrest and three week imprisonment after that experience certainly radicalized him further. Plagued by a quick temper, an indifference to business procedure (one student spent a day on the books and found customers had not been billed in four months), and an inability to tolerate the shortcomings of his highly creative staff, Garson threw in the sponge in June 1969 after eighteen months of publishing. Before Garson quit, however, the *Good Times* had attracted many of the Bay Area's finest writing and photographic talents. Marjorie Heins, Todd Gitlin, and Lenny Heller, along with Garson, were four of the finest reporters on movement activities in the country, while Nacio Jan Brown and Jeff Blankfort brought to the *Good Times* some of the most artistic front-page pictures on the West Coast. Bob Novick founded the *Good Times* with Garson but, finding the relationship with Garson too unpredictable and exasperating to tolerate, left after a year for an ocean retreat in Northern California. With Garson and Novick gone, the paper lost its driving force and the new staff began creating a rather different personality for the *Good Times*. Lack of financial stability is the death of many underground papers and, unless some steadier business person than was on the scene in early 1970 comes forth, the *Good Times* might be marked for oblivion as was East Lansing's *Paper*, Los Angeles' *Open City*, and the Los Angeles and San Francisco *Oracles*. Whatever the future of *Good Times*, it proved that underground papers can present graphics as effectively as slick magazines.

In May, a clique of liberal intellectuals headed by graduate student Bill Biggin started the *Temple Free Press*, which later became the *Philadelphia Free Press*.

In March, the seasoned author and journalist John Wilcock started his own *Other Scenes* in Los Angeles as an extension of the column he once wrote for the *Village Voice*. Wilcock had at one time been a reporter for the *London Daily Mirror*, the *Daily Mail*, the *Village Voice* and, most prestigiously, for the *New York Times*.

Other Scenes has really been another scene in the development of underground newspapers. In constant global motion writing

"How To Travel" books for Arthur Frommer Publishing Company, *Other Scenes'* founder John Wilcock never camps in one place very long. Consequently he has produced his bimonthly tabloid from Greece, London, Tokyo, Hong Kong, Los Angeles, and New York. A driving force in the development of many important underground operations (*Voice, EVO, Freep,* Underground Press Syndicate) Wilcock has his own typesetting facilities in New York City and makes enough profit from commercial printing projects to support *Other Scenes. Other Scenes* is unquestionably the most international of American underground papers and also has the added dimension of being produced by a foreign journalist. Reared in Great Britain, Wilcock admits, "I still get stoned by supermarkets, juke boxes and the boob tube." He was instrumental in founding the Underground Press Syndicate and is one of the leading policy-makers in the modern American underground press. A 1969 issue of *Other Scenes* explained the plans for "the first hippy daily," described in chapter fourteen of this book.

The *Rat*, a newspaper of "subterranean news" is also published in New York City and made a 1969 summer arrangement with *Other Scenes* to publish on alternate Thursdays rather than on a weekly basis to get some relief during July and August. *Rat* was founded in September by Jeff Shero, an ex-officer of the radical Students for a Democratic Society, to fill a void left by *EVO* which was getting away from radical politics and into underground poetry, comics, and scatology. The writing in the *Rat* is generally good with Jon Grell and Paul Samberg handling much of the live news reporting. The rock music section offers current information on who's playing where, with longer articles on individual groups. *Rat's* founder, Shero, who also helped start the Texas-based *Rag*, is a good example of being an activist first and a journalist only incidentally. Always heavily involved in radical politics nationally, Shero thinks nothing of catching a plane to Chicago, Denver, or San Francisco when movement activities occur in those areas. Shero said he started *Rat* when he stopped off in New York

City to visit some movement friends on his way back from a European vacation. The friends convinced him that the Village Voice was overground, the East Village Other was something "other" than politically radical, and Guardian was a national movement publication, so that New York City needed a radical political paper. Shero agreed, unpacked his bags, and New York has had Rat ever since.

Old Mole started in Cambridge, Massachusetts as a philosophical journal in September 1968. Not particularly notable for its graphics, the Old Mole takes its name from the Marxian quotation:

> We recognize our old friend, our old mole, who knows so well how to work underground, suddenly to appear: THE REVOLUTION.[14]

Old Mole is close to the Harvard University scene and although staffed largely by campus and community drop-outs, the content reflects the intellectual sophistication of the Harvard atmosphere. Old Mole has come to adhere rather closely to the SDS view of American society and now can usually be understood editorially as an arm of that organization. It received some national attention when it printed a group of letters taken from confidential files of Harvard during the SDS occupation of an administration building in March 1968.

Hard Times and the Chicago Journalism Review both started publication in October and are perhaps the most direct reaction to unexciting traditional journalism in America. Neither publication pushes experimental art work, sexual freedom, or subjective first-person reporting, but both do an outstanding job of anticipatory, analytical reporting.

The Chicago Journalism Review is a candid monthly critique of the city's press. It grew out of a feeling by many young reporters that their papers were too chummy with the government and the police during the Democratic Convention in 1968. Don Dorfman, formerly the education editor for the Chicago American (now

Chicago Today), quit that paper in the spring of 1969 to become full time managing editor of the *Review*. The circulation started at 500 and was up to 5,000 at 50¢ a copy by the summer of 1969. In one issue the *Review* charged that the *Chicago American* had interviewed a police department higher-up about the convention disorders then let him edit the story before publishing, a procedure considered a breach of integrity on any newspaper and one tantamount to censorship. Many reporters from Chicago dailies contribute to the *Review* and have not been reprimanded by their supervisors although one *Daily News* editor said, "I think the reporters for the *News* could be more constructive by channeling their criticism within the paper."[15] Many reporters with a penchant for investigative reporting disagree and the *Review* has been their medium for disagreement.

Hard Times is a Washington-based weekly produced by two real pros from the journalism field. The founders are Andrew Kopkind who has been with *Time* magazine, the *Statesman*, and the *New Republic*, and James Ridgeway who has written for the *Wall Street Journal*, *New Republic*, and the *New York Times*. The 7-by-11-inch, type-heavy weekly is sort of a radical *I. F. Stone Newsletter*, but is superbly written with carefully researched articles on many national problems. Ridgeway wants *Hard Times* to be "a buffer against the American capitalistic system," while Kopkind says, "It's not underground; it is not counter-culture; it's not counter-politics. . . ." Yet it covers many of the same stories as underground newspapers with a typical issue including in-depth reports on "Depopulants," "Defoliants," and "Drugs." *Hard Times* runs no pictures, obscenity, or advertising, and invites only top movement reporters to its columns. They sell their 5,000 copies mostly by subscription at $7.50 per year and list the modern exposé artist, Ralph Nader, on their masthead as a consulting editor.

No daily underground paper has ever lasted long. However, the Diggers in San Francisco's Haight-Ashbury produced *Free City News* for a three-month period during the Vietnam summer of 1967. Their 3,000 mimeographed sheets came out once or twice a day depending on local developments and were circulated free to people in the street. The 1969 People's Park incident in Berkeley brought another attempt at daily publication when an activist political group calling themselves the People's Press Syndicate produced *Instant News Service* for thirteen days. The People's Park incident involved a piece of land owned by the University of California and made into a park by Berkeley's street and hippy element without University approval. Police and national guard troops moved in to guard a fence built around the land, killed one person and injured several. During the ensuing thirteen-day siege, *Instant News Service* distributed 12,000 copies of the 11-by-17-inch folded sheet informing the demonstrators of survival areas, types of tear gas being used on them, locations for hospital care, and an anti-police interpretation of events.

There is no historical map for a road that has never been traveled. That is why no very sound predictions can be made about the future of underground newspapers in America. It is true that many of them die a sudden death after one or two issues while others like the *Village Voice*, the Los Angeles *Free Press*, and the *East Village Other* seem to flourish as the youth movement struggle continues. Because many of the educated young movement people believe in the possibilities of freedom of the press and are eager to use American journalism to inform the electorate from their own radical-left point of view, the underground press continues to sprout new papers for every one that grows irrelevant and dies. If government repression and police harassment of staffers on papers like the *Washington Free Press*, *Rat*, and the *Black Panther* continue, then the more radical papers like these will truly go underground. "Truly underground" will mean you won't be able to find out where it was printed or when you can get another copy. The staffers of such papers have already learned most of the skills necessary to publish from attics, basements, farm houses, and garages. The *Philadelphia Free Press* was banned at Penn State College's major campuses and radical students replaced it with the *Water Tunnel State College Free Press*. In Southern California, *Open City* folded while two journalism students from Los Angeles City College started *Image*. In Michigan the *Paper* ceased publication while the *Ann Arbor Argus* and *Fifth Estate* increased their circulation to take up the slack. As staff instability tottered Chicago's *Seed*, *Second City* began and *Kaleidoscope* came down from Milwaukee to keep the underground moving. In Texas where repression is high, Thorne Dryer of the Liberation News Service left New York City to start *Space City Times* and perpetuate the underground press in the Southwest. In Atlanta the *Great Speckled Bird* continues to publish a colorful, radical weekly in the face of persistent southern prejudice. In Boston the *Avatar* goes on a magazine trip and *Broadside* comes out with a bigger and more widely circulated underground paper. All across the country underground and movement newspapers are ending and beginning. Freedom is contagious and young journalists are spreading the antiestablishment word in underground publications on high school and college campuses, on military bases, in city ghettoes, the suburbs, or any place where a young, alienated audience needs communication with its peers. The underground press in America has become the visible expression of cultural revolution in America.

The new journalism in America was not started directly or indirectly by the *Village Voice*, by the Students for a Democratic Society or by a new breed of children raised by permissive parents. The underground press in America is one result of the prevailing conditions in American society. As long as the conditions in that society include a war long supported by the overground press, a population allowed to poison the air and water, to kill the cities and to oppress the poor, then this writer believes that the underground press will continue to flourish. And as long as America's leaders offer police repression and harassment as their chief answer to massive youthful unrest, the underground press may prove to be the only medium in the American society with the personal and economic freedom to question and challenge the Establishment—and to record the time historically from a youthful point of view.

3 / The Graphic Revolution

In Psychedelic Rainbows

*The new media is too important to be left to
the Peter Pan and Mother Goose executives, but
. . . (as a new art form) . . . can only be
trusted to the new artists.*

— MARSHALL McLUHAN[1]

In the five short years from 1961 to 1966 the beat generation had switched from coffee houses to parks, its members slept in communes not hotel rooms and found graphic expression for their life style in tabloid newspapers not little magazines. It was an opening up and a breaking out of the restrictions of the black and white beatnik era, and two underground publications, the *San Francisco Oracle* and the *East Village Other*, expressed the breakthrough with more inventiveness and imagination than any underground publications before or since. Allan Cohen, one of the founders of the *Oracle*, observed, "The *Oracle* was not planned, it was discovered." The discovery was American youth finding themselves, and the underground revolution in graphics was the printed expression of that discovery. When readers first paged through the *Oracle*, the psychedelic effect of soft blending colors appealed to and turned on their visual senses. (Plate 4) Michael Bowen, who was a member of the first *Oracle* Cooperative Publishing Association, had seen color used imaginatively on the front page of an issue of the *East Village Other* and convinced Cohen, Gabe Katz, an advertising agency drop-out, and Steve Levine, *Oracle's* managing editor, of its relevance to the turned-on San Francisco Haight-Ashbury scene. Writing about the *Oracle's* illuminated graphics in *Editor & Publisher* magazine, Ethel Romm boasted,

> Each Oracle page is designed as a composition first. The decorative area is given to an artist while the prose, or poetry, goes to the typist to set patiently on Varitype inside the pattern drawn. The text floats up the page in bubbles. Or it pours out in fountains. Colors blush over the page. . . . If only city hall news looked like this, I might read it.[2]

By 1966 Haight-Ashbury had become a haven for artists, poets, flower children, and many of America's runaways. *Oracle's* objective was to use the newspaper format as a voice for those involved in the new life of psychedelics and art. Consequently, little regard was paid to traditional black and white, greyed-out newspaper patterns. (Plate 5) In the *Editor & Publisher* item, Mrs. Romm, whose husband is the publisher of the daily Middletown, New York *Times Herald-Record*, declared:

> . . . [The psychedelic papers] make a standard newspaper look, to me at least, about as exciting as the telephone white pages.[3]

East Village Other in New York City, although not as psychedelic as *Oracle*, was equally experimental and a year ahead of the San Francisco publication. The first issue of *EVO* was an eight-page tabloid that unfolded into a long strip of paper. Allan Katzman, one of the paper's founders, explained that *EVO* was in competition not with other newspapers but with the highly visual television screen. Subsequent issues of *EVO* had to be unwound, pulled apart like an accordion, or put together as the editors experimented with new ways to work within the newspaper format.

Vertical and horizontal column and cut-off rules were eliminated as the *Oracle* and *EVO* stood the newspaper format on its head and tipped it sideways, running colors, art work, illustrations, poetry, and prophesy any way they felt was both artistic and appropriate to the message. *Oracle's* imaginative designers were the first to discover the split-fountain possibilities of the four-unit offset press, and issues nine through twelve of their paper were produced with six and eight colors bled and registered together. In short, the *Oracle* looked like a psychedelic rainbow while *EVO* changed its format from week to week as editors Katzman and Bowart did everything but print on brown paper lunch bags. Papers like *EVO*, *Oracle*, and the *San Francisco Express-Times*, which appeal to the visual senses and emphasize appearance over content, are referred to as "head" papers. The political papers like *Washington Free Press* and *New Left Notes* are ugly by comparison, with their message set in type and laid out in the most expedient manner.

In order to understand how the graphic revolution evolved it is necessary to trace the growth of offset printing to 1966. By then, offset reproduction with its multiple publishing centers and inexpensive, easy-to-operate cold type composition equipment had made the publishing of small newspapers financially feasible for anyone with a few hundred dollars and a political or personal cause. In the late 1940s or middle 50s, a journalism or political science graduate who wanted to enter the newspaper business as a publister would usually thumb through the classified advertisements in *Publishers' Auxiliary* or *Editor & Publisher* to find a dying letterpress weekly for $2,000 or $3,000 down. Bank money was generally tight for beginning publications and an adventurous young publisher had to have a bankroll, a windfall, or a rich aunt to get started.

There are two essential differences between the letterpress and offset printing processes that relate to the production of underground newspapers. The first is the relatively easy to learn technical skills required to produce a paper by the offset process. The second is the relatively small investment required to begin production on an offset paper.

The technical differences between the two processes need not concern us here. The important point is that in the present-day affluent American society, the offset process has made it possible for almost anyone to start his own newspaper. All a person needs, if he is so inclined, is an IBM typewriter with interchangeable typefaces, a lot of art work (cartoons, photographs, drawings, illustrations), and an urge to express his or her social, political, or cultural point of view. Once he is ready to begin production he types the news stories in columns approximately the size that will appear in the paper. The lines will be ragged on the right or unjustified; however, with a little more expense the lines can be even or justified. The *San Francisco Oracle* took artistic advantage of unjustified or ragged right lines by running copy to fit around pictures, line art, and psychedelic drawings. It is interesting to note that a few years after underground newspapers experimented with this method, sophisticated overground publications like *Vogue, Playboy*, and *Cavalier* began running unjustified, ragged-right copy blocks for artistic effect.

Next, headlines are set with a throwaway Pres-Type sheet, an inexpensive headline setting machine or by hand-drawn letters. When John Bryan started *Open City Press* in San Francisco in late 1964, he bought a case of metal monotype, hand-set lines as required, and simply pulled a proof to paste down for offset reproduction. It soon became cumbersome and time-consuming to redistribute each letter in the type case however, so Bryan switched to paste-down letters for his headlines. These letters rub easily into place like a dry transfer, come in a wide range of type faces, and cost less than two dollars for each 8½-by-11-inch sheet. Some papers like the Berkeley *Tribe*, the Chicago *Seed*, and the Bloomington, Indiana, *Spectator* draw in many headlines and display lines for local advertising by hand. This creates an intentional free-form flavor. If the papers want to look more professional, they pick up headlines or words from any printed pieces available. When an underground paper has enough capital, which is rare, it purchases a photographic headline setter. These machines set headlines one letter at a time by means of a photographic negative. Printed on a glossy paper, the lines can easily be cut out and pasted into place. Headline machines cost between $400–$1,000 for those who can afford them. After an underground paper is published for six months or a year, staff members often become more technically sophisticated and begin using an automatic waxing machine which places an adhesive backing on news columns and art work, eliminating the dirty job of gluing each item into place. These machines cost less than $400 and are easily maintained.

After the development of offset printing, cold type composition is the most important technical innovation utilized by the new left press. One advantage of cold type composition is in the keyboard. Letterpress typesetting on the Linotype or Intertype keyboard requires a six- to twelve-month training period, whereas the standard typewriter keyboard of offset composing machines can be used by almost anyone who can type.

Often more willing to share expenses and equipment than their competitive overground counterparts, underground production directors have established typesetting centers available to all movement papers. In San Francisco the *Good Times* once supplied the composing facilities for no less than six Bay Area underground publications. And in New York the *Guardian* and *Other Scenes* advertise and make available typesetting facilities for all area underground publications. Leasing of IBM Selectric typesetting equipment runs approximately $150 per month, including maintenance and repairs, while one new Linotype or Intertype machine for letterpress typesetting costs nearly $20,000 installed. Linotype and Intertype companies do not ordinarily lease equipment.

After all of his copy is ready for the camera, the fledgling underground publisher simply rubber cements, or waxes, his copy blocks and art work to layout sheets and he is ready to go to the printer. No underground newspapers have yet been able to afford the tremendously expensive investment in its own printing equipment, although a few have tried unsuccessfully. Liberation News Service (LNS) and FRED, two multigraphed underground news services with circulations under 500, actually printed on their own small presses, but they are graphically simple productions that run no color and few halftone pictures. The *Los Angeles Free Press* leased an entire printing plant in late 1969 when negotiations to purchase its own equipment failed.

The organizational key to the great proliferation of underground papers over the past decade has been the development of multiple publishing centers across the nation. These centers began as commercial printers. In the late 1950s, Meihle-Goss-Dexter, one of the world's largest manufacturers of printing presses and folding equipment, started a sales push on its suburban web-fed offset press. The cost of this four-unit printing press was nearly $20,000 per unit and most small publishers could not afford the $100,000 or so investment required to get it installed and running. Consequently, small overground printers and publishers grouped together to purchase the equipment, often forming separate corporations to handle the printing end of their publishing operations. Because most traditional weekly publishers are just as headstrong and individualistic as their underground counterparts, many of them found it difficult to work out the chain of command or the final authority for these joint ventures. Other foreign and domestic press manufacturers entered the field and financing loosened enough that small publishers and printers were able to plunge in to buy their own expensive equipment. Because it is financially impractical to maintain a piece of $100,000 printing equipment for a single publication, small publishers sought new accounts to fill their "open" press time. Suddenly all publications—over- as well as underground—were fair game.

In San Francisco, three such multiple plants handle some twenty-five underground publications, along with a hundred overground shoppers, advertising flyers, and weekly periodicals. One plant which handles the irreverent, 85,000 circulation Berkeley *Barb* also prints the *Catholic Monitor*. In Los Angeles, the forty-eight-page, 95,000 circulation *Press* is printed on two Fairchild Color Kings with seven units each, now leased by *Freep*. In the northwest, an overground weekly publisher prints the colorful *Helix*, *Northwest Passage*, and anything else he can get his hands on to help him make a financial go of it. In Wisconsin one courageous printer handles all editions (Chicago, Milwaukee, Madison) of *Kaleidoscope*, Chicago's colorful *Seed*, Wisconsin's *Counterpoint*, *Bauls of the Brickyard*, and a handful of independent high school publications. When local businessmen boycotted the advertising columns of the publisher's regular overground newspapers in an attempt to stop the printing of the underground papers, the publisher cited freedom of the press and argued, "I don't think a printer should deny his facilities to a justifiable use, a proper use, a legal use."[4] Finding printers for the politically radical and often abrasive underground press continues to be a problem, but as long as commercial printers have open press time on their expensive four-, five- and six-unit offset press equipment, underground publishers will find printers for their publications.

Necessity is still the mother of invention and much of the innovative graphic art in underground papers stems from their general lack of funds. Among the politically radical underground papers there is an unspoken principle that a paper cannot be politically effective and fiscally secure at the same time. Overground publishers become dependent upon their advertisers, the undergrounders believe, and sooner or later that dependence affects their editorial product. The problem with freedom from economic considerations is that only exceptionally well-done publications stay in business more than a year or two. Many never make it to the second issue.

While the *Oracle* was attempting to capture the new audience who had come "to San Francisco with flowers in their hair," Walter Bowart and Allan Katzman were experimenting in their own workshop with New York's *East Village Other*. (Plate 6) Bowart, one of *EVO*'s founders, was perhaps the first artist on the underground scene to experiment with the newspaper as an art form.

Bowart and Katzman founded *EVO* over a year before the *Oracle* was "discovered" and, although *EVO* was never as wildly colorful as the *Oracle*, it did many memorable graphically innovative things within the newspaper format. Screening and overlaying a photo of President Johnson's head on a Nazi storm trooper's body was a typical front-page picture for the bizarre and culturally radical Bowart and Katzman. Cartoons expressing blatant new left editorial messages was another first for *EVO*'s editors who wanted more than anything to shock their 65,000 subscribers to attention. Montages and collages of drawings and photographs were standard bill of fare for the earlier *EVOs* although by 1969 they had switched heavily into classified ads (Wheel and Deal) emphasizing people seeking sex partners, one- and two-page cartoon spreads and single-incident, hand-drawn front pages.

Helix in Seattle, the *Great Speckled Bird* in Atlanta, and *Other Scenes* and *Rat* in New York City run center spreads and four-page features in dazzling color on "How To Survive In The System," "How To Turn on Without Dropping Out," and "How To Follow The Youth Movement," because the offset process has made color economically feasible. The relative lack of large display advertising in such papers frees space for graphic experimentation.

Photographic experimentation with halftone overlays on line work, distortion and texture changes, screens of black and white solids and reverses have achieved many imaginative effects in the underground papers. The *Oracle* once ran a full-page photo of male and female nudes facing each other with the woman's back to the camera. They then overlaid a photo of a psychedelic table cloth in soft blues, purples and yellows. The effect was so dramatic that this symbolic image of the love generation was ultimately made into a poster which sold thousands of copies at $1.50 each. (Plate 7) The effectiveness of using white space liberally was discovered in full front-page pictures with screens dropped out from behind black panthers, fists, caricatured government leaders, and cartoons.

A testimony to the flexibility and innovativeness of underground graphics was a 1969, twenty-page summer issue of *Other Scenes* which consisted of sixteen blank pages with a colorful center spread announcing, "A Do-It-Yourself Newspaper Contest, First Prize—$250."[5] (Plate 8) Overground publishers carefully calculate the size and cost of white space used as a border around the print and to run sixteen pages of white space would be considered economic squandering if not insane. Such flexibility and versatility is characteristic of underground staffers who want, more than anything, to be free generally from the strictures of the American social system and free specifically from the economic and artistic restrictions of old fashioned newspaper graphics. *Other Scenes* printed only 10,000 copies (they ordinarily run 25,000) of the "Do-It-Yourself" newspaper contest issue but it was nearly sold out the second day on the newsstands. The issue also served to attract new talent to the underground press around New York City. Another example of the underground's creative imagination in graphics is the development of a Do-It-Yourself printing press kit by the editors of a military underground paper. The kit is called the "Benjamin Franklin Printing Press Kit" and is mailed to GIs who want to produce their own underground mimeographed messages. The kits are easy-to-handle, handmade operations consisting of a roller, ink, chemicals, sponges, duplicator paper, spirit memo carbons, and a 10-by-14-inch bed. The kits have been mailed free to servicemen in Vietnam and Korea, and in late summer 1969, manufacturing was planned to continue as long as requests kept coming in.

When *Good Times, Avatar, Seed,* the *Oracle* or *East Village Other* are mentioned by students of the underground press, it is usually in appreciation of some unusually effective graphic presentation. This is not to suggest that all underground publications are graphically well-balanced, artistically prepared, or even attractive. Quite the contrary. The majority of underground newspapers look more like the Berkeley *Barb* which has been called "the world's ugliest newspaper." Publications like the prestigious *Village*

Voice, the journalistically aggressive Los Angeles *Free Press*, or the extremely well-written *Hard Times* continue to stress the written word and are as graphically unimaginative and type-heavy as the *New York Times*. Other underground papers that have none of the literary brilliance of the *Voice*, *Freep*, or *Hard Times* look and read as if the editors were on a bad drug or alcohol trip when they prepared the material for the printer. Misspelled words, unnumbered or misnumbered pages, and captionless pictures are common to many of the more amateur underground papers. The significant point, however, is not that these papers are graphically ugly but rather that they are graphically possible. (Plate 9)

Tom Forcade of the Underground Press Syndicate in Phoenix, Arizona, estimates that an active publishing group can produce 3,000 copies of a black and white, eight-page, tabloid newspaper for $100. There are papers in this study which printed their first issue for less than $75. The days are gone when trade unions and expensive letterpress printing equipment made it impossible for political and cultural revolutionaries to get into the newspaper business.

Many of the new underground newspaper staffers are artistically inclined, college trained and highly skilled in the arts of graphic reproduction. They learn quickly, have none of the union restrictions about specialization and can operate typesetting, photographic, and addressing equipment with equal ease and agility. The old cumbersome, costly letterpress equipment is part of the past and young graphic designers not only don't miss it—they are not aware it ever existed.

Most of the papers begin with less than $500 capitalization and most improve graphically as the directors learn how to utilize the new processes. In the early days of printing in America a young man trained for five or ten years to become a tradesman or craftsman. The new breed of publishers in the underground press are changing much of the terminology in graphics and yesterday's "craftsmen" have become today's "graphic artists."

A Liberation News Service packet in March 1969 had this bit by Thorne Dryer:

> Every day millions of sheets of gray print come off the big commercial presses of America. Every day these gray sheets find their way into American homes, American minds. But into this sea of gray came a colorful splash—the underground press.[6]

Allan Cohen and his staff of poets, artists and prophets wanted to make the *San Francisco Oracle* "A graphic expression of man's highest ideals: music, art, ideas, prophesy, poetry and the expansion of consciousness through drugs." Graphically, the *Oracle* made a very colorful splash. The revolution in graphics in the underground press looked more like a psychedelic rainbow.

4 / Youthful Unrest

One Cause

How many roads must a man walk down,
before they call him a man?

—BOB DYLAN[1]

Anyone knowing the whereabouts of Shirley Carrigan
call her parents collect in Philadephia. 787-7840.

San Francisco Oracle

* * *

Sharon, please get in touch. It will be so different
at home. Call me collect, am so worried. Mom.

East Village Other

* * *

Gale Erlich—Please come home. We love you and miss
you. Call 408-243-7965 or San Jose Switch Board.

Berkeley Barb

HUNDREDS OF SIMILAR ADVERTISEMENTS RUN weekly in the classified columns of underground papers across the country. What causes American youngsters to run away, to become hippies, yippies, drug users, and social dropouts? What has happened to the home, the church and the school in American society that suddenly even stay-at-home youths are protesting, demonstrating, and rejecting the very institutions under which they are raised? Like the underground newspapers they read, these people are products of a world built by their parents. They live under government leaders they did not elect, pay taxes that support a war they detest, and attend schools chosen for them and administered largely by authority figures they cannot accept.

When a young man leaves the cocoon of the American home he finds out quickly who runs the world. At eighteen or nineteen he may have all the intellectual, emotional, and physical abilities he will ever have and is considered adult in every respect but one. The law says he isn't until he is twenty-one. Who says twenty-one is the magic age of maturity? Certainly not the American military establishment! They say he is a man when he is eighteen. One ancient argument for the 21-year-old coming of age is that, until then, a person hasn't enough experience for voting responsibility and determining his own destiny. If "experience" is any criterion, today's young people accumulate more experience in the global village of television in their first eighteen years than many of their parents have in a lifetime.

So as the young people of today venture forth in the adult world prepared for them by their parents, they find their freedoms and their powers to determine their own destiny greatly limited. They also find that real world vastly different from the idyllic one studied in history and social science text books. When the high school and college freedom riders bussed to the American Southland to protest racial oppression they found inequality to be an American reality. These morally-awakened young people found the war in Vietnam untenable, the befouled air and water and the choked-up cities unacceptable, and the relative indifference of America's political leaders to these problems to be cause for unrest and protest.

The gap between professed ideals and American reality as they experienced it proved ultimately to be the cause of much of the forthcoming opposition to American established authority. The cause of youthful unrest was not just a simple divergence between McLuhan's technological society and antiquated schools, churches, and governmental bodies. It was also moral indignation toward a nation that could make a hero of former Nazi U-2 rocket scientist Wernher Von Braun for contributing to America's billion dollar space program, while sending David Harris, an articulate American intellectual, to jail for three years because he resisted the military draft that would send him to kill Vietnamese people. Young Americans were rejecting parents who consumed more coffee, alcohol, and tobacco than any American generation in history. They began to ridicule parents who, while raising them in an atmosphere of violence and drugs, put them down for smoking pot and turning on to electronic rock music.

Explanations of contemporary unrest range from "too-permissive" child training attributed to the influence of Dr. Benjamin Spock to the wildly radical Students for a Democratic Society of Tom Hayden to the neo-Marxist revolutionary philosophy of Dr. Herbert Marcuse. Rebellion against a university system that treats young adults as children; rejection of the consumer society and what it stands for; disillusionment with the competitiveness and hypocritical standards that characterize our times; the battle for civil rights; and revolution "for the hell of it;" these are just a few of the broad causes mentioned for youthful unrest.

The revolution is cross-national, however, and began in 1956 with revolts in Hungary and Poland, the wave of Existentialism in France, Marxism in Great Britain, and the Beatniks in America. The common characteristic of these movements was that they derived their momentum from youth-power. Their targets were almost always universities, governments, or other institutional authorities, which is why trouble often began on campuses.

Young people have tried to play the establishment's game by the establishment's rules but the results have a tendency to favor the establishment. When University of California law students marched on Sacramento to peacefully protest police intervention in university affairs, the Governor was "too busy" to meet with them. When a band of thirteen New York parents made a formal written request to a school principal supporting their children's plan to publish an independent newspaper with "no obscenity," the principal's reply was, "I feel compelled to refuse you the right to distribute *Frox* [the name of the paper] as you request and must advise you that any violation will lead to disciplinary procedures."[2] Young Americans peacefully oppose the war in Vietnam and their patriotism is impugned; students unanimously resent the Selective Service System yet the draft continues.

Young people who were old enough to fight in a war they did not create, but not old enough to vote for the leaders who prosecuted that war, began in the 1960s to inquire critically about the foundations of the society they were to inherit. Many of them considered the "straight press" part of that establishment and no longer believed in it.

John Wilcock, a former staff member of the United Press International and the *New York Times*, wrote in his own underground paper, *Other Scenes:*

> There is a credibility gap between the press and the people, because the newspaper owners are plain and simple liars. They have fostered wars and want the people to believe that the Viet Nam war is a holy war. As a result, the Hippies just don't read the national papers.[3]

The high school and college pop-gun press that addresses itself to class elections, litter on the campus, and poor attendance at school athletic events is not only often out of touch, but helps create an atmosphere which encourages the new communication of the underground papers on campus.

Meanwhile youthful unrest has nurtured a network of some 3,000 regularly and irregularly published underground high school papers, many of which are simple one-page mimeographed sheets.

The students who run them are most often not classroom failures. Tom Lindsay, one of the founders of the High School Independent Press Service (HIPS) which offered a weekly packet of news for some 200 high school papers and 250 subscribers in 1968, is a high school drop-out who found class assignments irrelevant. Jon Grell, who handles news for *Rat* on New York City's teeming East Side is an 18-year-old graduate of the highly selective Bronx High School of Science. Richard Cohen moved into a New York ghetto commune from Greensboro, North Carolina, because his father, a successful shoe sales executive, disapproved of his organizing Peace vigils at his southern high school. All of these young men are articulate, bright, and turned off by the American system of education.

The silent generation of the Eisenhower 50s used to sit around rapping about how they could capitalize on the leisure that was surely coming from automation, cybernation, and the advanced technology of the electronic age. They expected the new generation to engage in boating, golfing, fishing, camping, dating, and dancing, and just generally enjoy the new-found American affluence. Little did they realize the new generation would want to do something besides drink beer, go to dances, and rush for fraternities. How could they foresee that the young people would want more relevant education and more responsive leadership in the country? The new generation reacted to the establishment's monolithic status quo stance by sitting in, being in, loving in, demonstrating, demanding, confronting and even occasionally blowing up and burning down the institutions controlling them; namely, schools, big business, and the government. College administrators were slow to learn that college students wanted to have a voice in what and how they learned. Business leaders could not cope with graduates who wanted something to say about company policy, and big government was too immobilized by bureaucracy to deal effectively with poverty, discrimination, or antiquated draft laws.

The present American youthquake was not anticipated; and thus Americans were not ready for the revolution of human energy that was upon them. The unpreparedness of the silent generation was at least part of the cause of the student and protest movements.

The four media which are most responsible for the youthful revolution are music, films, television, and the underground press.

Every revolutionary movement in modern American history marched to some tune or other. The American Revolution whistled "Yankee Doodle;" the Civil War boomed "John Brown's Body;" World War I stepped to "It's a Long Way to Tipperary;" World War II sang the lonely "Lili Marlene." The sound of the youth movement was introduced by Elvis Presley's grinding, pounding "You Ain't Nuthin' but a Hound Dog," which set the movement's rocky tone. Over the past fifteen years there has been a steady evolution to California Rock, New York Rock, Acid Rock, the British Beatle Rock and raga rock, with all the soul music of Negro Americans' rhythm and blues underlying the topical musical message. Protesters, prophets, and troubadours brought psychedelic electric sounds to the movement while America's young wore Indian costumes, Western pants, and long hair. They stamped, stormed and sang, "We Shall Overcome," "The Times They Are A-Changin'," and ". . . something is happening here but you don't know what it is, do you, Mr. Jones?" in participational youthful unity.

Ron Fabin wrote in the Establishment's *Kaiser Aluminum News* "Children of Change": "The sound of music is, indeed, the sound of revolution."[4] Dob Dylan, Phil Ochs, Joan Baez, and the Jefferson Airplane provided the impetus and the movement shifted from love songs to radical politics and the rejection of the American establishment.

If music was the sound of the new generation, films and movies were most certainly the sight. The television babies had grown up with a medium that involved them in the action-packed world outside the TV living room. Young people refused to accept being entertained as captive movie goers. As McLuhan had taught them, "They were not an audience. They gave an audience to the screen." They wanted to participate in the action—to be involved.

Kodak and Ansco had made it possible for ten-year-olds to make home movies, while inexpensive Japanese radios made it possible for seven-year-olds to carry their transistors to school. Because of film and TV, the younger generation were more closely involved in the assassination of President John F. Kennedy and Martin Luther King, Jr. than with their high school principal or college president. And as they attended schools filled with books and words, they begged for films and pictures. To them the novel was quickly becoming a suspect art form, the short story a further attempt to take them out of reality, and the conventional word, a symbol of a dying culture.

Anthony Schillaci wrote in a *Saturday Review* dedicated to "The New Movie":

> The young are digging the strong humanism of the current film renaissance and allowing its currents to carry them to a level deeper than that reached by previous generations. One might almost say that young people are going to the film maker's work for values that they have looked for in vain from the social, political or religious establishments.[5]

That is why Standard Oil, the government under the Kennedy administration, and sophisticated church organizations produced films in an attempt to make contact with America's young.

Television is so much written and talked about as the cause of youthful unrest, it is almost informational overload to include it here. Nevertheless, TV probably has more to do with the impatience and short concentration span of America's young than any other single source. Youth who is constantly barraged by instantaneous new products, new services, and new entertainment cannot understand why it takes so long to get equality for oppressed peoples, enough food and shelter for the poor, or changes in outdated draft and voting laws.

Music turned them on, television tuned them in, film got them involved, and the underground press gave rebellious American youth the voice they sought to express its new-found awareness.

Against their parents, the police, the university, the government, the status quo, or anything else that symbolized authority over their lives, America's impatient, instant generation sought a medium that would favor legalization of marijuana, free love, self-determination for all peoples, and racial equality. Given a new generation, a new sound, a new vision, a new sexuality, a new hope, and a new cynicism, the new medium—the underground press —was inevitable.

Critical of the production-oriented motives of acquisitiveness, competition and aggression of their parents, the collective psyche of American youth seeks a new set of motives. They believe the motives of their parents are outdated and drive people to lead lives less human. They wish to be driven by love, the desire to educate relationships, and the desire for new knowledge. The allegedly upside-down value system of the Establishment motivates many of the young activists in their opposition to American social institutions, putting them on the frontier of the change or shift in America's cultural consciousness. They are not as concerned as their parents with earning money or making profits. They want to be "groovy," to "dig each other," to "give power to the people," to be "right on" in politics and with drugs, and to be in charge or ahead of the culture they believe is dying. Youngerground people are not the new frontier in sex or politics, but they may well foreshadow America's life styles over the next ten or twenty years. A revolution changes people's life styles, usually radically.

According to John Galbraith's *New Industrial State*, the jobs of 7 or 8 per cent of the American work force will be eliminated by automation within the next ten years.[6] The workers unneeded in production will be involved in doing the things necessary to educate themselves and their relationships with one another. Leisure is the trend and people will have more and more of it. Thus competition, acquisitiveness, and aggressiveness will be, in a sense, programmed out of the citizens of tomorrow. In this writer's opinion, much of the strain and pressure in society today exists because the older generations who helped build the country are not willing to accept the conditions created by the technology they developed.

The underground press talks about new experiences in sexuality. Its editors show pictures of people having sexual intercourse with one another and have the directness to call it "fucking." They introduce sexual freedom without guilt. They complain openly and strenuously about the aggression of police, about the acquisitiveness of our corporate structures, about the sickening competitiveness in our colleges, and they complain about the dehumanizing effects these national characteristics have on all people. They refuse much advertising because they believe advertising teaches us to exploit one another.

As the underground press looks at America's leaders in 1970 what do they see? A country that remains silent when reactionary forces suppress free people in Greece and the Dominican Republic, under the guise of democracy and anticommunism. A society that complacently allows its cities to decay and become increasingly polarized into largely white, affluent suburbs and teeming inner-city concentrations of poor. A society that is unable to think of any better response to the youthful protest and unrest flowing from these conditions than police repression. A society that poisons itself by polluting its countryside, its water, and even the air it breathes. A San Francisco librarian observed sadly in an article on the American youth movement that when he meets older people who can't understand the terrible young people who rebel and protest and want to change the society, he is forced to admit that he just doesn't understand the *older* generation.[7]

Who are America's alienated and unrestful young? Observers who write about children of change as the exclusive products of affluence don't really understand the scope of the American youth movement. America's unrestful young are everywhere and they come from everywhere. Kids from New York, Boston, Detroit, Denver, Dallas, Los Angeles, Seattle, and San Francisco are turning away from the society of plastic swimming pools and cement cities. Rich kids, poor kids, black kids, brown kids and used-to-be kids are questioning the values of America's social and political systems. Puerto Ricans in Chicago form their street gangs to protect themselves against the MAN. Fort Worth college drop-outs move to New Mexico to join communes to get away from IBM cards. Philosophy students in Massachusetts leave the universities to join the Forte Hill Communications Center in an attempt to avoid the dead-end, diluted life that threatens to sap their psychic and ascetic energies. What they all share is a profound conviction that the places from which they came impose an intellectually and emotionally sterile set of conditions that makes it exceedingly difficult for them ever to get to know themselves. And they don't necessarily have any answers to the problems they did not create.

The lesson to be learned from the turbulent youthquake is not that long hair or body odor or disrepect for traditional values are undermining the stability of America. The lesson for America is that something is terribly wrong with the systems that create such youthful unrest. And who are the most outspoken critics of these systems? Pick up an underground newspaper in Ann Arbor, Michigan, Jackson, Mississippi, Middle Earth, Iowa, New York, Chicago, or Los Angeles. One might find they are trying to tell America "what is happening . . . Mr. Jones".

5 / Radical Politics

Another Cause

*Those who make peaceful revolution impossible
make violent revolution inevitable.*

—JOHN FITZGERALD KENNEDY[1]

The UNDERGROUND PRESS IN MODERN AMERICA HAS, from the beginning, been the voice of opposition to sluggish cultural and bureaucratic political institutions. That it turned abruptly in 1967 from an expression of flower-child love, participatory rock music, and occult religion to coverage of campus unrest, police confrontation, and radical politics further testifies that its nature is to react to the pressures on its young readership. Flower children were thrown in jail for sitting on the pavement in San Francisco, rock musicians were arrested for possession of marijuana in New York City, and underground journalists were beaten and busted for reporting activities of the youth movement all across the country. As the politics of alienation matured through struggle into a dawning revolutionary consciousness, the underground press slowly changed from a reflection of the isolated hippie phenomenon into the self-conscious agent of radical politics.

The change was not permanent.

One explanation of the pendulum-like swing from cultural to

political emphasis in the underground press from 1967 to 1969 was given by a director of *Avatar*, who described the shift as part of man's natural cycle from inward, withdrawn spiritual considerations to outward, involved political interests. *Avatar* claimed to be entering the cultural or meditative phase of the cycle in late 1968 when it switched from newspaper to magazine format and began emphasizing religion, contemplation, and self-knowledge. *Avatar* proved to be at least eighteen months ahead of the rest of the underground press who, in late 1968, were just getting up a head of political steam. The growth of the new left press from a handful of scattered weeklies in New York, Detroit, Berkeley, Los Angeles, and Austin in 1965 to over 450 papers by 1969 was largely a result of the outward politicalization of the American youth movement.

It is no easy matter to trace or define America's radical political movement, since its members seem to have neither blueprint nor party line to guide them. The common bond, or fundamental unifier, has been that all of the organizations are made up basically of young Americans rising up against the old. There is a widespread feeling that the older generation has failed, the young no longer respect them, and the consequence is rebellion. Margaret Mead points out in her new book, *Culture and Commitment*, "It is not only that parents are no longer guides, but that there are no guides"[2]—and youth, being the principal inheritors of the new age, have as much to teach as to learn.

Perhaps the group that best depicts the alliance of youthful rebels is the Chicago-based Students for a Democratic Society (SDS). Although troubled by much factional infighting which naturally results when politically motivated youth tries to organize, SDS has been the movement's most significant national organization.

SDS was organized in 1961 in Port Huron, Michigan, and proclaimed in its first manifesto that it would seek

> ... a democracy of individual participation, governed by two central aims: that the individual share in those social decisions determining the quality and direction of his life; that society

Radical Politics   61

> be organized to encourage independence in men and provide
> the media for this common participation.[3]

Individualism is inherently opposed to collectivism, and the singular insistence on individuality in that statement has perhaps been the reason for much of SDS's inability to tie the youth movement in America together.

In the beginning, SDS was a coalition of liberals and radicals working for a new perspective on peace and disarmament, civil rights, university reform, and poverty. They even supported the pre-Gene McCarthy Democratic party and sold buttons saying, "Part of the Way with LBJ," but the bitter experience of the 1968 Chicago Convention moved them radically away from their original left-liberal stance. By 1969 SDS had adopted a position totally opposed to anything and everything Establishmentarian. At the chaotic Chicago Convention, SDS adopted what was known as "The weatherman proposal," named after a line in Bob Dylan's "Subterranean Homesick Blues" in which he sings, "You don't need a weatherman to know which way the wind blows." The proposal called for the government's withdrawal of all U.S. troops from Vietnam, and for elimination of the draft, racism, and the universities' affiliation with big business and government.

Perhaps more significant than that resolution was SDS's inability to incorporate all of the important youth groups under the SDS banner. At the 1969 convention SDS expelled the well-organized and powerful Progressive Labor Party (PL), because PL rejected the Black Panther party's revolutionary nationalist ideology. One Black Panther spokesman warned PL, "If you can't relate to Huey Newton then you can close up the red book." One month after SDS had aligned themselves with the Panthers, SDS National Secretary, Mark Rudd, was badly beaten by an unidentified gang at the Panther-sponsored United Front Against Fascism conference in Oakland, California.

Whatever the divisiveness within SDS and the movement, SDS claimed some 70,000 dues-paying members at $5 a year, located in 350 chapters, mostly on or near college campuses. And so as one edge of SDS seemed to lose its chances to serve as a centralizing political agency, the other edge gained enough national publicity to widen the notoriety and scope of the movement. SDS has published its own official newspaper, *New Left Notes*, since 1965 and maintains a strong influence over such widely-circulated publications as *Rat, The Old Mole, Philadelphia Free Press, Washington Free Press*, and *Rag*, along with the influential Liberation News Service.

Most of the radical political organizations in the youth movement are loosely affiliated and free-form in structure. Two such groups are the antidraft organizations called Resist and Resistance.

Resist was formed in 1967 by a group of professors and social critics including MIT"s, Noam Chomsky and author Paul Goodman. Most of Resist's 350 members belong to faculties of universities and are organized around a peace and antidraft position. Resistance was started by a younger group of draft resisters on the West Coast and involved itself with personal witness types of antidraft demonstrations. The public burning and handing in of draft cards, refusing to be inducted, and arranging for campus draft counselors are some of the activities of this officerless and nonstructured group. David Harris, one of Resistance's founders and most notable members (he is married to folk singer Joan Baez and was the former president of the student body at Stanford University) is serving a three-year sentence for refusing to be inducted.

Another significant, politically radical organization, the National Mobilization Committee to End the War in Viet Nam, or MOBE as it is called, was first founded to coordinate various student groups at the 1968 National Democratic Convention. Rennie Davis, one of those indicted for conspiracy against the U.S. Government at the Chicago Convention was MOBE's first national coordinator and Tom Hayden, SDS's first president, helped Davis develop its national movement projects.

A smaller umbrella group, but one that could replace SDS as

the vanguard of the movement, is the New University Conference (NUC) formed in Chicago in March 1968 by a national group of teachers and graduate students. Expanded in 1969 to include 600 campuses, NUC originates most of its activities on the local level, a practice that appeals to those opposed to the doctrinaire approach of SDS. Another somewhat radical youth organization in 1969 was the Washington-headquartered National Student Association. NSA was unable to reach the radical majority because over the previous ten years it had been funded by the U.S. Government, which most radicals consider to be the enemy. Once NSA was disaffiliated from government funding, its large membership was eligible and were expected to join forces with the radical political movement. Its organizational network could possibly be a key to future coordination of youthful radical politics—or it could simply continue as a kind of travel agency that coordinates trips for students to places throughout the world.

Many other loosely allied youth groups have developed nationally to react to and generally oppose American capitalism. Among the most notable are the World Student Union (WSU) and Youth Student Alliance (YSA), the Black Panthers, Progressive Labor, Peace and Freedom Party, Women's Liberation, and the W.E.B. Dubois Club, the latter a direct extension of the Communist Party in the United States.

While these national organizations continue to perpetuate non-structured coalitions, many ghetto-oriented, big-city based street gangs joined the movement as part of "the people." As the 1969 SDS statement suggested: "The overturn of power from the elite will take the movement's whole strength and that strength lies in the power of the people."[4] Black-jacketed motorcyclists joined hands with university radicals, Southern high school students responded to black and brown causes in the cities, and Women's Liberation joined the movement as something other than a support group for radical male activists.

Women's Liberation staged their own demonstration at the Miss America pageant in Atlantic City and, according to an article in the *Spectator*, "flung bras, girdles, steno pads and dish cloths into a Freedom Trashcan."[5] Women's Liberation attacked the "Pussy Power" jokes of Eldridge Cleaver and the "only position for women in SNCC is prone" slogan of Stokeley Carmichael as smug male chauvinism. Tired of being marketed and packaged by the male-dominated American "free" enterprise system and of being seen as sex objects, the radical women see themselves as oppressed not only by a sick economic system but also by a history of personal suppression similar to that applied to blacks in America. At the Underground Press Syndicate conference at Ann Arbor, Michigan, the following resolutions were passed by voice vote:

> 1. That male supremacy and chauvinism be eliminated from the contents of the underground papers. For example, papers should stop accepting commercial advertising that uses women's bodies to sell records and other products, and advertisements for sex, since the use of sex as a commodity specially oppresses women in this country. Also, women's bodies should not be exploited in the papers for the purpose of increasing circulation.
>
> 2. That papers make a particular effort to publish material on women's oppression and liberation with the entire contents of the paper.
>
> 3. That women have a full role in all the functions of the staffs of underground papers.[6]

As the Vietnam war politicized and alienated a growing number of people on the fringe of radical politics, the underground press reacted with a similar politicalization. And as the papers shifted from psychedelics to confrontation politics, a new breed of politically-educated activist-oriented journalists changed the tone of the new medium.

The *Philadelphia Fress Press* was initially a quiet voice on the Temple University campus reporting only on college issues. Originally an unimaginative, pictureless two-page paper, the *Free Press* grew under doctoral candidate Bill Biggins and his activist staff to a colorful sixteen-page format including coverage of local, state, and national movement news. The *Guardian*, formerly a dull, old left weekly has also undergone a political and youthful transformation. Carl Davidson's political coverage "From the New Left," Margie Stamberg on women's liberation news, and Todd Gitlin's reporting of confrontation politics comprise some of the finest writing in the movement press and makes the *Guardian* a colorful paper.

In San Francisco the *Movement* has grown from a two-page mimeographed Northern California arm of the Student Nonviolent Coordinating Committee (SNCC) into a carefully-edited monthly analysis of the radical political scene. Antidraft, civil rights, culture and the media, and Vietnam are all covered live and in depth in the *Movement*. The *Guardian* in New York and the *Movement* in San Francisco distribute nationally and address a more sophisticated movement audience than most regional underground publications.

The San Francisco *Good Times* became vibrantly radical under the direction of Marvin Garson and included imaginative layouts and perceptive analytical reporting on the turbulent Bay Area campus situation by Margie Heins, Lennie Heller, and Garson. Before founders Bob Novick and Garson split, *Good Times* was considered one of the best papers in the movement. Many other papers including *Rat* in New York City, the *Great Speckled Bird* in Atlanta, and *Kaleidoscope* in Milwaukee have changed radically since the politicalization of the youth movement.

As was mentioned earlier in this chapter the shift from cultural to political emphasis in the underground press was not permanent. By 1969 many underground editors were disillusioned and depressed by the failure of the Peace and Freedom Party, SDS, or the Black Panthers to get the youth movement together. High school students in particular were disdainful of SDS's depersonalized structure and believed high school problems to be too regionalized for solution by SDS's doctrinaire resolutions.

Many of the underground press's leaders had given up on cities, schools, and American institutions in general and were trying alternative ways of living—particularly in communes across the country. Timothy Leary, an early guru in the psychedelic movement believed that over one million dropped-out young people were living in communes in the United States and Europe by late 1969, and *Newsweek* called it the year of the commune.

One-time editors from San Francisco's *Good Times* and *Oracle*, Chicago's *Seed*, and New York's Liberation News Service had given up on chances of living fruitfully in modern-day American cities. They now lived in California, Massachusetts, and Arizona farm areas and believed themselves to be significant victims standing on the edge of a dying civilization, no longer willing to report the inanities of a country turned on to plastic and concrete.

The new breed of underground editors were tired of being maced and clubbed and teargassed by the police. Word was out in the movement that the battle could not be won in the streets where "The MAN" had all the weapons. *Fifth Estate* in Detroit turned its editorial attention to the joys of rock music, *Rat* in New York City and *Peninsula Observer* in Palo Alto, California, spoke to the problems of ecology, *Free Press* in Los Angeles concentrated on the cultural arts, *Seed*, *Planet*, and *Good Times* pushed for the legalization of marijuana.

The underground press in America defies categorization. As soon as one labels it "cultural" it moves toward politics, and as soon as one records the shift to politics, it swings back to cultural. It is never purely political or cultural at any one time.

The strength of any revolution is determined by the quality of its leadership and that quality is gauged by its ability to rally significant support at crucial times. Participants in peace marches and campus confrontations have numbered in the thousands and those who dismiss the movement because only 2 per cent are involved sadly miss the point in the exercise of youthful power. Some leaders like Jerry Rubin, Abbie Hoffman, Paul Krassner, and Tom Hayden seem to thrive on providing opposition to the MAN, while other leaders crop up across the country to replace those who have dropped out. Marvin Garson of San Francisco's *Good Times* reported in a statement announcing his retirement as editor that

"Nothing Lasts."[7] Many of his staffers claimed he would be back, however, which gets us back to the "inward-outward" theory of Boston's *Avatar*. As America's underground editors move inwardly they address themselves to the spiritual concepts of Buddha, Christ, and Confucius. As they move in that direction, the underground press takes on the cultural-religious tone of poetry, psychedelic art, and astrology. As they shift outwardly into the world, confrontation politics, police harassment, and student unrest fill their columns and pages.

Whatever radical politics failed to accomplish for youthful or national unity, the nation must acknowledge with painful honesty that many questions were opened to serious discussion and debate by the radical political movement of the 60s. To have made it politically safe and profitable for the moderate forces in American public life to take up these issues is a service that future historians may well record with gratitude.

What has been written on the preceding pages on radical politics and youthful unrest is at best a sketchy account of these two significant American phenomena. They have been touched upon only because they are obvious causes of the growth in underground papers. No claim to thoroughness is intended or implied since these phenomena are incredibly complex and amorphous. For a vastly more comprehensive explanation of youthful unrest or radical politics, the author refers the reader to Kenneth Kenniston's brilliant *Young Radicals* or Lewis Feuer's insightful *The Conflict of the Generations: The Character and Significance of Student Movements*.[8]

Youthful unrest in America has been created largely in reaction to institutions which fail to cope adequately with the problems perceived by the young. The emergence of radical politics in the past decade is the tumultuous evidence that traditional American politics are out of touch with large masses of those young. And whether the pendulum swings toward the political or cultural revolution, the underground press seems to be the clearest expression of what is going on.

6 / Underground News Services

The Associated Press It Ain't

The Underground press is like 300 fingers.
What we need is to make one fist out of those 300 fingers.

—TOM FORCADE[1]

THE IDEA FOR SOME SORT OF AN ALLIANCE OF UNDER-
ground papers was conceived in the offices of the *East Village
Other* in June 1966. Walter Bowart and John Wilcock are generally considered the founders of the first such alliance, the Underground Press Syndicate; but Bob Rudnick and Allan and Donald
Katzman, then staffers at *EVO*, also helped organize UPS. The
Katzmans wrote some of the first position papers for a press service,
Bowart attended the first national convention for UPS, and Rudnick was its first coordinator.

A June 15, 1966 editorial in *EVO* written by Allan Katzman
suggested the following proposals for an underground press syndicate:

1. *Communication of the news that the middle-class press won't
print or can't find.*

2. *Some sort of teletype service between New York, Chicago,
L.A., San Francisco, England, etc.*

3. *Dividing of all income between members.*

4. *A clearing house, where members can choose to syndicate other members' by-lines, columns and comic strips.*

5. *An advertising agency which will represent and produce advertising for all members from sources around the country.*

6. *An agent for all member newspapers to the whole communications industry to represent them and sell news for them to A.P., U.P.I., radio and television networks.*[2]

Nine months later on the Easter weekend, UPS held its first national meeting at Stinson Beach, California, a refuge for creative drop-outs, hippies, and members of the San Francisco Bay Area drug set. The major papers represented at that first beachside meeting were New York City's *EVO*, Berkeley *Barb*, *Los Angeles Free Press*, *Los Angeles Provo*, *Rag* (Austin, Texas), *Washington Independent*, San Francisco *Oracle*, and Chicago's *Seed*. Other UPS members at the time were *Underground* (Arlington, Virginia), *The Paper* (East Lansing, Michigan), *Guerrilla* (Detroit), the *Eagle* (Washington, D.C.), *WIN* (New York City), *Peace News* (London), *Sanity* (Montreal), *Peace Brain* (Chicago), *Prometheus* (Eggertsville, New York), *Satyrday* (Toronto), *Art and Artists* (London), *Canadian Free Press* (Ottawa), the *Illustrated Paper* (Mendocino, California), and *The Fifth Estate* (Detroit).

The three qualifications for membership in UPS were that 1) all members agree to free exchange of materials, 2) all members agree to occasionally print a list of UPS members and, that 3) all members agree to exchange subscriptions gratis. The first rule of UPS is perhaps its most significant and served to break down the concept of copyright among underground papers from the start. Rock music critic John Sinclair wrote in the UPS Directory:

> . . . the formation of UPS really broke down the obsolete and horrible copyright scene. Who says the words belong to us? How did we get to own them? Copyright is just another bullshit Western ego trip and a capitalistic greed-scheme. Nobody can own the fucking words, and it's a good thing, too. Like I used

to tell the band when they'd forget—music is always free.
. . . It's just in the air, and so are the words.[3]

This sharing is similar to the overground Associated Press in that AP members can pick up news from one another, although AP charges its membership for the privilege.

Other than leaving the organization of UPS up to *East Village Other*, not much was accomplished during that first beachside meeting. No decisions were reached on leadership, financing, or general organization—which is possibly why the first stages of UPS were so unsatisfactory to the membership. Taken over largely by *EVO* and coordinated by *EVO* staffer Bob Rudnick, UPS did little during its first year. Upset by UPS's inability to allocate monies for advertising placed through the Syndicate, many members blamed Rudnick and *EVO*. Thus in March 1968, Rudnick handed the gavel over to John Wilcock, by then publishing his own underground paper, *Other Scenes*.

The first problem for Wilcock was to get financing which he quickly did by setting up a subscription system for libraries at $50 to $100 a year, wherein participants received one-year subscriptions to UPS member papers. According to Wilcock the drive netted $3,000 after which he persuaded Tom Forcade to handle the organizational end of UPS in Phoeniz, Arizona.

In one short year, the energetic Forcade formed a corporation, arranged for a national advertising representative, compiled an underground press directory, put together a permanent library of underground periodicals, books, and films, and started *Orpheus*, an underground monthly magazine. By 1969 UPS was serving as a general clearing house for inquiries from its members, interested scholars, and the public in general.

If Bowart, the Katzmans, and Wilcock were the kickoff team for UPS, Forcade had become the ball carrier. Very much concened with structure and law, Forcade conducted the business of UPS with a tightly-regimented groups of five or six people, only one of whom was paid a regular salary. In 1969 that salaried person was Virginia Norton, UPS's secretary and she received $20 a week. UPS operated out of an old house near Phoenix's capital district until September 1969, at which time it moved to New York City. It owns a 1946 Chevrolet school bus which serves as a mobile filing cabinet for the staff when they attend underground press conferences.

A major contribution of UPS to its membership was the formation of Concert Hall Publications in Glenside, Pennsylvania. It serves as an advertising representative for seventy-nine of the top underground newspapers in the country. Staffed by Bert Cohen and Michael Foreman, Concert Hall, according to Forcade, was placing nearly $40,000 a month in advertising insertions in underground papers by the summer of 1969. Marvin Garson formerly of San Francisco's *Good Times*, said of Concert Hall, "If they went out of business, fifty underground papers would go down with them." Concert Hall solicits advertising exclusively for undergrounders from record companies, camping equipment firms, motor bike makers, and men's clothing manufacturers.

From Phoenix, UPS published a directory containing ad rates, subscription prices, distribution information, printing techniques, and general news from the underground. Also produced is an irregularly published newsletter containing information from member papers, a financial report, and general advice on how to solve legal and financial problems. UPS maintains an underground distributing agency and puts new underground publishers in touch with likely retail outlets and printers in each region. UPS members pay a $25 initiation fee and there are no dues.

Orpheus magazine, published by Forcade and the Phoenix group, is a representative collection of articles from underground papers with more emphasis on culture than radical politics. It is sort of a *Reader's Digest* for the new left and runs lots of color, both in inks and papers, and stresses the films, music, and theater of the underground. With a stated circulation of 24,000 *Orpheus* claims to be a "Bi-monthly collection," although it comes closer to circulating quarterly. *Orpheus* is a nonprofit organization and is not corporately connected to UPS.

Until 1969 UPS was controlled by an elected coordinating group made up of Wilcock, Abe Peck, then with Chicago's *Seed*, Art Kunkin of the Los Angeles *Free Press*, and Jeff Shero of New York's *Rat*.

At the 1969 summer convention at Ann Arbor, Michigan, UPS changed its structure to a participating democracy with Forcade and Wilcock assuming most of the responsibility. During that meeting participants discussed distribution, advertising, printing, business management, and legal problems and how to solve them. The major action was distribution of a mimeographed proposal by Forcade appealing to the overground press for support of the underground's constitutional right to freedom of the press.

An important point about UPS is that it is *not* a news service but rather a combination of a library clearing house, a publishing company, and an advertising representative for the underground press. It might be likened to the overground American Newspaper Publishers Association plus the *Publishers Auxiliary* plus the American Newspaper Representatives.

While UPS is similar to the Associated Press in structure, the Liberation News Service in New York City has been compared to the overground's United Press International. LNS provides its members with twice-weekly packets including news stories, essays, poetry, photography, and underground comics. The information is gathered by a network of underground reporters, photographers, and cartoonists mainly in the United States and has approximately 500 subscribers. One hundred and fifty of these subscribers are underground publications, the other 350 are made up of "straights" or establishment subscribers.

A typical LNS packet includes news of a college strike, a trial of draft-resisters, a new insurgency by the Saigon government, a report on black rebellion from southern schools, a book review on movement activities, and photographs sympathetic to students and members of the political new left. A subscription to LNS costs $15 per month if you are a member of the underground press and up to $1,000 if you are the *New York Times*. The *New York Times* does not subscribe but the Columbia Broadcasting System and *Look* magazine do, and Doubleday Publishing commissioned LNS to do a book on the Columbia University dispute in 1968. LNS had the only media representatives inside Columbia during the confrontation and provided the only first-hand account of that incident.[4]

If it is a slow week politically in the movement, LNS may feature long, analytical articles, whereas if it is the week of an SDS convention or a campus revolt of national significance, the packets will have a greater number of shorter entries.

LNS was founded in Washington, D.C., in 1967 by Ray Mungo (Boston University, '67) and Marshall Bloom (Amherst, '66), both radical editors of their college papers. According to LNS, Bloom was to be the director of the United States Student Press Association (USSPA), a liberal group of college editors, but was purged because he was considered politically radical. The need for an underground news service had already been widely recognized at UPS meetings and LNS was to become the central nervous system of the underground press. In the early Washington days, LNS related to the movement primarily as an extension of the hip, tumultuous youth culture and featured a far wider and more colorful range of news and information. Shortly after LNS moved to New York City in spring 1968, a bitter factional dispute developed among its staff. The dispute was vastly complex, but generally the Bloom faction wanted to remain cultural and colorful while their opponents wanted to get more heavily involved with SDS and radical politics. During the summer Bloom took the printing equipment and some monies raised from a benefit and moved LNS to a farmhouse near Montague, Massachusetts. A short-lived operation was formed—it ceased publication in January 1969. Jesse Kornbluth wrote of the group's demise, "We're writing more creative words, as opposed to reporting other people's inanities." Kornbluth published an anthology of underground writing for Viking Press, *Notes From the New Underground*. Depressed over a pending jail sentence for draft evasion, Bloom took his own life in November 1969.

Stunned by the Massachusetts defection, broke, and without printing equipment, the New York group picked up the pieces and formed a fourteen-man collective that was intent on providing a service emphasizing a radical interpretation of American institutions and politics. Many movement editors believe LNS slowly formed a mafioso-type alliance with SDS and vice versa. During the 1969 SDS Convention in Chicago, the entire LNS staff attended, leaving no one in New York to mind the news desks.

After it swung so heavily to revolutionary politics, LNS lost much of the lightness, humor, and color of its earlier days, although it is perhaps more politically effective since the shift to revolutionary politics. The packets are printed on awkward 11-by-14½-inch sheets presented in straight type with little or no imagination or taste for graphics. A major contribution of LNS to the underground press movement is that their substantial packets of radical political news make it possible for many short-handed underground staffs to fill up their columns. Although this is a "filler" or "boilerplate" technique, many beginning new left publications need the LNS service to get started.

LNS and UPS are the most notable national unifiers for the underground press, but there are other less publicized groups that should be mentioned. One such group is the now-defunct High School Independent Press Service (HIPS), started in the fall 1968 in the offices of LNS. A group of fifteen New York City high school editors had conceived the idea the previous spring as a strictly New York City thing. Most prominent among them were Howie Swerdloff, Paul Steiner, Jon Grell, Tom Lindsay, Robbie Newton, and Dave Graham. Graham kept the idea alive over the summer, and by fall had compiled a mailing list of sixty papers and some four hundred student supporters. HIPS subscription rates were $2 per month to high school independent papers and

$4 to all others, over or underground. They were obviously influenced by LNS whose equipment and office space they shared and their news packets were similar to LNS' in tone, if not in content. HIPS concentrated on high school issues such as dress codes, behavior policies, and expulsions, but soon became radicalized by their experience with police during the New York teacher strikes and by the suppression of independent high school papers. HIPS was very much involved with revolutionary politics in January 1969, when they discovered it took all of their time preparing the biweekly packets. The last packet had an explanation of the difficulty of meeting deadlines which read, "We won't go into a rap about why we haven't come out for a month. Suffice it to say that we didn't print a packet last week, or the week before, or the week before that."[5] Unable to see the relationship between SDS's doctrinaire philosophy and the New York high school scene, one HIPS staffer told this writer, "Those people (SDS) don't understand the problems of kids in New York City. We gotta work our own problems out and HIPS takes too much of our time." Part of HIPS former staff publishes the twelve-page, 40,000 circulation biweekly *New York High School Free Press* and had no plans in 1969 to get back into the independent high school press service business. The *New York High School Free Press* is distributed free and is supported by advertising and contributions from benefactors.

Shortly after HIPS ceased publication in New York City, another high school oriented group started a larger, more thorough underground news service called simply *FRED* in Chicago. *FRED* was started in early February 1969 by Clark Kissinger, Lowen Berman, and Harriet Stulman. According to Kissinger, *FRED's* purpose is "to upgrade the writing in Chicago's many high school underground sheets." Subscription rates for the 48-page weekly service are $2 per month to poor organizations, $5 per month to "nonprofit media and less poor organizations" and $10 per month to commercial media. *FRED* had 250 subcribers in July 1969, set its own type and was printed by staffers on a mimeograph machine in a dilapidated second-story apartment. *FRED* is unattractively presented on 8½-by-11-inch sheets that are printed both sides and typewritten single spaced in monotonous seven-inch lines. Their coverage, however, ranges wide and is well written. One June 1969 issue included stories on Chicago's blacks, business, establishment politics, labor, law and order, movement harassment, poverty, schools, and legal survival information.[6] A Chicago distributor of many underground publications including *FRED* predicted the service would be short-lived "unless they get some financial help." Apparently no help came and *FRED* ceased publication in fall 1969.

Katzman's 1966 proposal for "some sort of teletype service" for the underground press was realized when in 1968 a wire service called the Underground News Service (UNS) set up telex connections in New York, Washington, Berkeley, and London as an extension of the Liberation News Service. The Berkeley *Barb* uses UNS for a by-line when someone sends in information requesting anonymity. *Barb* and LNS utilize the UNS wire occasionally and the *Barb* was the first West Coast publication to carry the Columbia University dispute as it was reported by LNS members inside Columbia.

The short-lived Student Communications Network (SCN) in Berkeley, California, was another attempt by radical activists to operate a news service. It was started in December 1967 by Howard Perdue, Orlando Ortiz, and Ken Olieari and was oriented to campus and students news. It folded after a few months when it failed to attract enough subscribers to support the operation.

Another organization that has had a unifying effect on West Coast underground publications is *Vocations for Social Change*, published every other month from Canyon, California. More cultural in tone, VSC is dedicated to "being helpful to people struggling with the fundamental question 'What am I going to do with my life?'"[7] VSC circulates its 48-page magazine-type monthly free to some 10,000 subscribers. In order to get more than one issue, however, readers must make a donation to "*Vocations for*

Social Change, Canyon, California 95416." They refer to themselves as "an impartial clearinghouse" but most of the information is aimed at radically changing the American establishment. Content offered by VSC includes news "Coordinating the Movement for Change," "Alternative Institutions," "Living Off the Fat of the Land," "Peace and the Draft," and "Job Openings in the Underground press." VSC is not in any sense a news service for underground papers, but is included here because it serves as a clearinghouse of ideas for new left editors and readers of the underground press.

The antimilitary, antiwar GI Press Service was started while a draft of this manuscript was being finished in mid-1969. Prepared by the Student Mobilization Committee to End The War in Vietnam, it distributes its sixteen-page, stapled, bimonthly releases to some thirty-five underground papers. Civilians pay 50¢ for a copy, servicemen 25¢, and annual subscription rates are $1 a year to GI's and $8.50 to civilians. Typical bill of fare for GI Press Service is: "The Cost of Commitment," a table listing 36,000 GI deaths since the war began, cartoons of Presidents Nixon and Johnson grilling American soldiers over a fire labeled "Hamburger Hill," and self-explanatory articles entitled, "Billions for War," "Guidance on Dissent," and "GI's View of Withdrawal." GI Press Service is produced in New York City by Allen Myers and other members of the student-oriented committee. It anticipates competition from the independent wing of military papers discussed in chapter twelve.[8]

Still another "news service" that pops up in scattered underground news stories is the Intergalactic World Brain. The IWB insignia was taken from Spain Rodriguez' underground comic strip, *Trashman*. The IWB by-line has been used in the Berkeley *Barb* as a joke or as a cover for a story whose source is meant to be confidential.

Underground press services are structured very much like underground newspapers—loosely, freely or not at all. They are short-lived, highly amorphous, and constantly ebbing and flowing with the needs of the new medium. By the time this information is in print, statistics on underground news services will undoubtedly have altered many times. Only last March (1970) there arrived the Free Ranger News Service (FRINS), a bimonthly packet produced by Tom Forcade and the Underground Press Syndicate in New York City. Similar to LNS offerings, FRINS is, however, more cultural than political. An April 1970 packet reflected, typically, the survival mentality of the culturally radical Forcade and included articles on "How Not To Get Burned," "How To Pirate Records," and a cover from the "Fabulous Furry Freak Brothers" comix.

Although many underground publications were founded to provide an alternative cultural or political voice, the significance of the new left press is that it is a movement. The string that ties the movement together has been the Underground Press Syndicate, the Liberation News Service, and the other cooperative agencies. As an added bonus for members, Tom Forcade of UPS reminds his membership, "The Underground Press Loves You."[9]

Present / Where It's At

7 / Economic Operation

Making the Bread

They have no business sense, so the printer has to be more than a printer and the distributor has to be more, too.

—An underground press printer

Politically radical underground newspaper editors operate on the principle that it is impossible to be fiscally sound and editorially free at the same time. This strongly anti-establishment maxim has been both the strength and weakness of the new medium and explains much of what underground papers have, and have not, been able to accomplish socially and journalistically.

The technological revolution in graphics has played a major economic role in the growth of underground papers over the past ten years. Aspiring young editors and politicos no longer had to start at the bottom on small dailies and work up. All they needed to start their own paper in the middle and late 60s was a carbon-ribbon typewriter, a jar of rubber cement, and $100 hustled from friends. Ten years earlier they would have needed to mortgage their parents' house, borrow from rich relatives, and give up their college education to get into the letterpress-dominated small newspaper business.

Ed Fancher of the *Village Voice*, the granddaddy of all undergrounders, claims his paper had to invest nearly $80,000 before it stopped losing money. The *Voice* was started in 1955 when investment capital for small publications was scarce and Fancher admitted, "It got so tight at one time I had to borrow $200 from my father to get the printer off our back." Times have certainly changed. The *Voice* now prints on two presses in separate locations with a weekly printing bill of nearly $14,000 and twenty-five full time people on the payroll. Radical underground publishers do not believe the *Voice*, the Los Angeles *Free Press*, or the *East Village Other*, all of whom have enough money to meet their weekly printing bill, have much effect on changing society. The dissident editors believe a publicaton begins to sell out to the establishment when it starts making money and they argue the content of the above-mentioned papers is relatively harmless to the establishment. Whatever their unpopularity among the less financially successful undergrounders, the directors of those three papers understand the economics of newspapering far better than their more radical underground brethren. For the most, however, these papers consistently, if not violently, oppose and criticize the American Establishment.

The Berkeley *Barb*, on the other hand, also made money until July 1969 despite its violent opposition to the institutions under which it operated. Covering every new establishment blunder or political upset, the *Barb*'s gross profits were estimated at $264,840. This estimate was published in the *Berkeley Fascist/Berkeley People's Paper*,[1] a two-in-one short-lived satirical newspaper published by Allan Coult, the Anthropology professor who purchased the *Barb* from founder Max Scherr. Coult estimated that Scherr was grossing almost $5,000 a week with the *Barb*. He purchased the paper for "an exceedingly fair price" (estimated at $200,000), according to a story in the "Barb Sold" issue in July 1969.[2] Scherr was reputedly stingy with his staff. His top editors got only nominal weekly wages while most staffers were paid the minimum $1.65 per hour or 25¢ a column inch. When Scherr founded the

Barb he wanted to call it the *Pinch Penney Pricker,* which, according to the disgruntled staff who left him to establish the *Tribe,* would have been a more appropriate name for the "Sheer Profit" *Barb.*

While the *Barb,* the *Voice, Freep,* and *EVO* need enormous sums to keep pace with weekly printing expenses, most underground papers operate on a total budget of $500–$1,000 per issue. The expenditures of the San Francisco *Good Times* with a press run of 12,000 copies is closer to the average underground newspaper— $20 per 1,000, sixteen-page paper plus $6.50 per page for negatives and plates. There is no make-ready charge for runs over 5,000, and a $35 base fee is charged for color plus $2.50 per 1,000. Most publishers in this study charge $50 base fee for color plus the $2.50 per 1,000. Thus the average printing bill for the publishers of *Good Times* is $350–$400 "up front" per issue unless they run color. "Up front" is a term used by printers of underground papers indicating they must be paid in advance of publication.

Office rental is usually under $100 per month with most publications operating in low-rent, depressed urban areas, out of upstairs apartments, garages, or dilapidated warehouses. *Other Scenes* in New York City and the *Ally* and the *Tribe* in Berkeley operate out of the homes of the editors as do many beginning publications. *Rat* in New York City paid $100 per month for its premises as did *Good Times* until word got out that the papers were unpopular with the local establishment. When the landlords doubled the rent, *Good Times* moved and *Rat* started looking for new office space.

An expense that sometimes exceeds production cost on some papers is the distribution and postal charges. Most underground papers have to mail first class since they cannot comply with second class regulations of the United States Post Office on obscenity. The second class privilege enjoyed by the *Voice, EVO,* and the Los Angeles *Freep* cuts the mailing costs to subscribers by almost 90 per cent. *The Ally* in Berkeley, California, is a military underground paper and cannot mail second class to its paid subscribers on military bases. Because of the strict mail inspection procedures at military installations only first class designation insures delivery of the highly volatile, antiPentagon *Ally*. The *Ally* hand-addresses some 2,500 of their 12,000 monthly papers and bulk mails the residual 9,500 to sympathizers near military bases. This distribution process costs *The Ally* nearly $400 per issue while only $186 is paid for printing.

Telephone bills are another major expense of the talkative underground press editors who think nothing of calling New York, Detroit, Atlanta, Saigon, or Algiers to dig up information or to arrange an impromptu meeting or movement happening. Phone bills range from $100 to $1,000 per month and the phone company is wary of papers who leave it "holding the bag" after a few hectic months of publishing.

Conventional distribution methods do not ordinarily work for underground papers since major distributors both nationally and regionally are unwilling to handle the inexperienced and troublesome new medium. There are thousands of titles looking for national distribution and, since there isn't room for all of them, distributors simply won't take the chance of getting busted for handling a financially risky, often "obscene" underground paper.

Most distributors' dollars come from large circulation magazines, widely distributed dailies, and cheap paperbacks. Even the daily newspapers are low-profit items, often handled only as traffic-builders or as a customer service.

Basically there are three distribution possibilities for any publication, under- or overground. The first possibility is the retail level, which, for underground publications, includes sympathetic bookstores, newsstands, head shops, liberal university student centers, and art museums.

The next possibility is the regional distributor. Major distributors carrying *Time*, *Playboy*, *Look* and *Newsweek* are generally conservative and susceptible to pressure from right wing organizations, and thus will not touch underground publications. Although some may carry *Rolling Stones* or the *Village Voice*, the risk of carrying underground publications would eliminate them as a distributing possibility if ideology and pressure didn't. One arrest for possession of obscene material can cost a distributor a week's profits.

Second line distributors who handle *Fling, Cuddle, Nudist Lover,* and some pornographic magazines will sometimes distribute the more popular underground newspapers. Every major city has one or two such distributors but their reliability is not high. According to Tom Forcade (UPS) "all distribution is shot through with dishonest, semidishonest, unreliable, inefficient and uncaring people." The publisher of the *Illustrated Paper* in Northern California said he bulkmailed 1,500 copies of his publication to New York City distributors; it was three months before he received any payment—a check for $20. He realized it was a losing proposition and discontinued the bulkmailing.

Both publishers and distributors in the underground are unreliable and care little about record keeping. *Good Times* in San Francisco, *Open City* in Los Angeles, and *Rat* in New York City hardly kept track of bulk distribution or whether national distributors pay for their shipments.

According to UPS, one of the most trusted secondary distributors in Los Angeles went out of business and left debts of $10,000 to Los Angeles' *Free Press,* $2,000 to *Horseshit* magazine, and $500 to UPS. Los Angeles with thousands of news outlets now has only one secondary distributor handling underground papers.

The standard price to the wholesaler is 50 per cent of the retail price. A national distributor will want 35–40 per cent of the cover price. The retailer in turn gets papers at about 80 per cent of the cover price and thus makes only a few pennies on each sale of a paper retailing for 15 or 20 cents. *Rolling Stones* is 35 cents, the irregularly published *Gambit* is 50 cents and the *American Avatar* is $1 a copy, but they are the exception to the rule.

Most secondary distributors in the United States can be identified only by letters such as J&J, B&M in New York City, L&S in San Francisco, or the UPSDA in Phoenix. The titles of companies like Gil Terry in Chicago, The Southern Subscription and Distributing Service in New Orleans, Morris Moskowitz in San Francisco, Irv O'Connell in Los Angeles, or Jones Distributing in Dallas may or may not be bona fide—some include fictitious names. Only a handful of cities have underground wholesalers who can make a living at distributing underground papers. Police harassment is great for such adventurous entrepreneurs and arrests for distributing obscene materials have taken place in Berkeley, San Francisco, Los Angeles, and New York. It is unrealistic for the underground press to think anyone is going to distribute its papers simply out of sympathy for the movement. The work is strenuous, low profit, anxiety provoking, and exhausting.

Morris Moskowitz (not fictitious) in the San Francisco Bay Area is one of the few sympathetic distributors, a rare breed. Known around the Bay Area as "Moe," Moskowitz owns a popular bookstore on Berkeley's Telegraph Avenue and has been arrested on charges of selling pornographic literature. He distributes the Chicago *Seed*, *East Village Other*, *Village Voice*, *Black Panther*, and *Other Scenes* in his store, and for awhile handled the *Good Times* distribution to vendors. Even "Moe" has doubts about the feasibility of distributing underground papers but when interviewed said, "I don't know what the future holds for them. I distribute them because I think it should be done. These kids are trying something new and it can't be done without good distribution. They have no business sense so the distributor has to be more than a distributor. I write them checks and sometimes they don't even cash them."

Once an underground paper becomes big enough or popular enough, conventional distributors *will* handle it. The *Free Press* in Los Angeles has over 600 outlets and the *Village Voice* in New York City sells approximately 60 per cent of its 130,000 circulation through newsstands.

Newsstand owners are traditionally liberal-minded, perhaps because they are used to being harassed for selling what some members of the community consider pornographic literature. Thus, the best distribution system for underground papers seems to be no system, with each paper making its own arrangements.

Underground papers are often distributed free, especially when they first start. Papers are handed out at political rallies, love-ins, be-ins, poetry readings, art festivals, light shows, and rock music concerts. The Philadelphia *Free Press* (circulation 25,000) and the *New York High School Free Press* give away all their papers free, getting the necessary income from advertising and benefactors. They have no subscribers but will mail copies to anyone who sends in an addressed and stamped envelope. *Helix* in Seattle, *Rat* in New York City, and *The Old Mole* in Cambridge, Massachusetts, sell their papers but distribute newsstand returns free to high school and college campuses to interest students in the political movement.

Politically-oriented publications such as the *Guardian* in New York City, the *Movement* in San Francisco, and the *Black Panther* in Oakland all use bulk mailing for their national distribution. The *Movement* distributes 20 per cent of its 20,000 monthlies nationwide, while the *Black Panther* puts out its 85,000 weekly papers through twenty-eight national Black Panther offices.

A second-class bulk mailing permit can be obtained from the United States Post Office for a $30 fee. This allows items weighing less than 2.618 ounces to be mailed for 3.6¢ per piece, and tabloid papers up to twenty-four pages ordinarily qualify. Second-class permits are available to regularly published legal newspapers with 65 per cent of their subscribers paid and less than 75 per cent of the content taken up by advertising. Brief lives and impatient editors prevent many underground papers from getting the second-class permit, and so they pay the 6-cent per copy first class fee. The expense mounts quickly when a publication grows to over 1,000 circulation.

Street sales have been highly successful for the Berkeley *Barb*. Each Thursday night some 200 hippie-type people hold *"Barb"* parties until around midnight or one o'clock then go to the *Barb* office to pick up their packages. They pay 7½ cents per paper in advance and usually buy 100 papers to sell for 15 cents each. Buyers often hand the vendors 25 cents, giving them a 10-cent tip, so that the sellers can earn about $10 with a bundle of 100 papers. *Barbs* sell notoriously well in Berkeley and, on a heavy traffic corner like Telegraph and Bancroft Way at the University entrance, sales vendors can sell a bundle in an hour. *Barb* prints around 85,000 with an average paid sale of 76,000. One week in November 1968 was typical, with 85,000 printed and 76,729 sold. The street sales kids are high school and college drop-outs, students, runaways, drug users, or anyone who needs to make $10 or $20 in a day. In talking to forty or fifty of the street sales people, this writer met young law and engineering school graduates, a former army officer, and even an ex-weekly overground newspaper publisher. They had all dropped out of society and needed to earn money without the problem of working for someone else.

The *Barb* averages 5 cents a copy from all circulation, which should net it about $2,500 a week. The *Barb* also carries nearly 40 per cent advertising at an open rate of $5.00 per column inch, which is above the average inch rate for underground papers.

Paid subscriptions represent only 10 to 15 per cent of the total circulation of most underground papers with the more established new left publications circulating closer to 40 per cent by paid subscriptions. Most rates are in the $5 per year range which leaves the paper with 3 or 4 cents per issue when postage and handling costs are subtracted. Newsstand and street sales net the paper closer to 6 or 7 cents per copy and *East Village Other*, according to editor Allan Katzman, gets 6½ cents up front, or in advance, for 60,000 of their 65,000 circulation from their distributor. *EVO* is more popular in New York City than other underground papers, as *Rat* and *Other Scenes* who net 5 cents on each copy sold. *Hard Times* in Washington, D.C., and the *Chicago Journalism Review* accept no advertising and exist on subscription income only. *Hard Times* charges $8.50 per year (forty-two weeks) and has 5,000 paid weekly subscribers, while *Chicago Journalism Review* has 5,000 paid monthly subscriptions at $5 per year.

Many publications have no expectations of longevity and simply sell by the copy. Prices of such publications range from 10 cents per copy for the *Sun* in Ann Arbor, Michigan, 15 cents for *News From Nowhere* in DeKalb, Illinois, to 50 cents for *Gambit* in Phoenix. Other more optimistic publications establish long-range rates such as *EVO* at $10 for two years, *Canada Goose* at $9 for two years, or *Liberation* at $18 for three years. A few papers offer a discount for servicemen or students, but most never bother with such details since they sell most of their papers through retail outlets and street vendors.

Most undergrounders carry something like 30 per cent advertising and 70 per cent editorial matter, with only the larger circulation papers attracting national advertising. The accounts solicited by Michael Forman and Bert Cohen of Concert Hall for the 79-member Underground Press Syndicate are mainly record companies featuring the underground sounds of rock and soul music. Robert Rolontz, Atlantic Records advertising man, says "A typical $5 album that needs 25,000 sales to break even gets a promotion budget of about $1,000 to $15,000 maximum."[3] This eliminates any possibility of ads on television or in major market magazines, so the logical medium becomes the underground press. Barry Morrison of Mitchell-Morrison, Inc., who handles ABC Records said, "You can run forty pages eight times in underground papers for what it would cost for one page in *Playboy*."[4]

Full page ad rates start at $40 for *Middle Earth*, and go all the way to $1,100 for the no longer very underground *Village Voice*. The *Voice* has its own advertising staff and representative, even employing a market analyst, Mark Clements Research, Inc., for sophisticated readership surveys.

Advertising in the underground press usually consists of small, hand-drawn notices of rock concerts, movement speeches, experimental or sex-oriented underground films, head shops selling hippie paraphernalia, avant garde book stores, sandalmakers, mod clothing stores, and psychedelic stores selling incense, cigaret papers, and imitation hashish.

Perhaps the easiest type of advertising for the underground press to attract are the sex-oriented classified ads. Classified ads like the following bring up to $6 per inch:

> *Incredibly straight male, 44, athletic, clean wants to meet lascivious, beautiful chick for sneaky-poo games. I look like something between Marlon Brando and Mickey Mouse with Montgomery Clift and Peter Lorre for cousins. Please lovely, lewd damsels, show me where your head is. Call——.*
> *Ask for 'Uptight.'*[5]

Paid-in-advance advertisements like these are hard to turn away when the printer demands his money in advance. One Los Angeles *Free Press* editor claimed, "We would like to phase them out but financially we can't exist without them." Allan Katzman of *EVO* has no compunction about running the sex mating ads and argues, "They perform an important service for the sexually frustrated and lonely New York readers who have no other advertising medium."

Most of the underground papers don't have the circulation to be represented by Concert Hall for the national ads and settle for whatever local advertising they can get.

A bugaboo of underground papers when trying to gain national advertising is the overall inconsistency in advertising rates among Underground Press Syndicate members. While *Helix* in Seattle with a circulation of 10,000 charged $250 for a full page ad, *Dwarfe* in Phoenix with an identical 10,000 circulation charged $100. North Carolina's *Anvil* charged $200 for a full page ad in their 5,000 circulation sheet, but for the same price a media buyer could get Milwaukee's *Kaleidoscope* with editions in Milwaukee, Chicago, and Madison, with a total circulation of 40,000.[6]

Opposition to any kind of standardization or conformity is characteristic of the dissident press and has become a real sales obstacle for Foreman and Cohen at Concert Hall. However, the general attitude of disinterest in the profit end of newspapering is central to the underground.

Salaries on underground newspapers are almost nonexistent, even on the more successful papers. EVO pays a handful of full-time staffers $45 a week, *Helix* in Seattle supplies eleven full-time people with food and lodging, while the *Rat* in New York City pays two or three full-timers $25 each "when we have it." *Distant Drummer* in Philalelphia and the Los Angeles *Free Press* are exceptions with well-paid staffers, but they are not considered "very underground" by most radical editors. *Distant Drummer* tries very hard to be like the *Village Voice* in content and had a weekly payroll of $1,000 in 1969, according to editor Don DiMaio; and the *Free Press* in Los Angeles has full-time employees earning up to $175 a week plus commissions in advertising. *Drummer* boasted of the amount of advertising in its columns and claimed to be the only newspaper in the underground with a sound business formula.

Since most underground staffers work on papers because of a basic disbelief in the American economic institutions they usually find other ways of supporting themselves. Most of these sources are establishment-oriented and overground. Paul Krassner of the *Realist* earns his living as film critic for *Cavalier* and society editor for *Ramparts*. One colorful secretary for the San Francisco *Oracle* filled in as a Kelly girl when she needed survival money. One editor of the irregularly published *Glebe* in central California is the news director for a local radio station, while Jon Grell of *Rat* earns his living writing about the movement for overground book publishers. *Rat's* advertising manager, Marvin Grafton, makes his bread publishing a scatological New York newspaper called *Pleasure*, while part of the income for EVO staffers comes from a monthly underground comic publication, *Gothic Blimp Works*, and a second New York sex paper, *Kiss*. In the summer of 1969 *Kiss* had a weekly newsstand sale of 70,000 at 35¢ cents, while *Blimp Works* was printing 25,000 monthlies at 25 cents.

Two other New York sex-oriented newspapers, *New York Review of Sex* and *Screw*, were started by ex-editors of the underground *New York Free Press* after that publication folded. *Screw* had reached a press run of 100,000 before New York authorities clamped down because of its blatant photos of sexual intercourse.

Underground editors do many unusual things to save money or get the bread (supplies) necessary for publication. Some underground editors encourage their women to shoplift clothes and supplies when they need them. Since they consider the business establishment to be exploitative and fundamentally immoral, they have no compunction in encouraging theft from the MAN. When the Diggers, a group of practical and aggressive Haight-Ashbury hippies, were producing their daily mimeographed *Free City News*, they often had girl friends employed by San Francisco offices as secretaries steal the duplicator paper to print on. Another underground paper had one of its staffers get a job with a printer as a plate maker so she could set the type for her paper on the printer's typesetting equipment after hours. Underground papers have student staffers and sympathizers pick up photographic equipment, dictionaries, copy paper, and art supplies from college publications (when the journalism adviser isn't looking); and one West Coast publisher reportedly made monthly trips to the black jack tables in Las Vegas and used the winnings to meet monthly publication expenses.

The militant, military *Ally* has had a steady stream of benefactors, many from college faculties, as had the well-written *Mid-Peninsula Observer* in Palo Alto, California. One group of attorneys pledged and delivered $3,000 to the *Ally* to help keep the antimilitary sheet in business. Already mentioned has been how the Berkeley *Barb* was originally financed by the sale of Max Scherr's bar, Steppenwolf, and how the book and record sales of *Macbird* by Barbara Garson helped finance the *Good Times* (*San Francisco Express-Times*).

Many notable establishment journalists contribute to the underground press, often without a fee. If William Burroughs writes a piece for *Esquire* his fee is sometimes over $500, whereas he will write similar articles for New York's *Rat* without charge. Rock critic Ralph J. Gleason contributed material to the radical

Liberation News Service while he earned his livelihood as a full-time *San Francisco Chronicle* music critic. Many old and new left journalsts contribute to the underground press colums. Allan Young, a *Washington Post* drop-out, is an LNS mainstay, while movement writers Jerry Rubin, Art Johnson, and Jim Schreiber have worked for established media.

Bookkeeping and accounting procedures are almost nonexistent on underground papers and some send out bills only if the spirit moves them. While researching this book, the present writer found checks for $24 and $4 at UPS in Phoenix on the floor next to an old desk and asked if they had been lost. "Oh forget 'em; God provides money whe we need it," was the casual response.

Necessary income for publication of some papers is provided by musical benefits, poster and button sales, and profits from underground books, magazines, and films. SDS gets income to publish *New Left Notes*, its weekly paper, from response to the two-page "SDS Lit List" of poems, books, posters, and films. These materials are available at wholesale prices in bulk quantities to other members of the underground movement. Trust runs low among underground editors and the SDS Lit List carries the following message: "Our policy is to fill orders only when payment is received in advance."[7]

In summary, the economic organization of underground publications becomes more overground as the publications grow in circulation and staff. They make the money necessary to pay the printer, the telephone company, and the distributor in any way they can. When they can't make payment, they cease publication temporarily—often permanently.

The underground press is unquestionably the least professional effort in the publishing business, but its proprietors claim their editorial strength lies in their seeming weakness. Unable to find advertisers to pay for one color, they go ahead and run six colors in one issue. Unconcerned with copyright laws and legal restrictions, they print any stories they get their hands on. Often excluded from second-class mailing privileges by the United States

Postal authorities, they print every obscenity and four-letter word in the book and some not yet in the book.

Many underground editors complain that *Village Voice, EVO* and the *Free Press* are just in it for the money. But, as Tom Forcade of UPS reasons, "No newspaper, not even the *New York Times*, publishes just for the money." Traditional overground publishers are aware of the power of the press and feel some responsibility to inform the readers. Congenitally opposed to the American free enterprise system, most underground staffers feel little responsibility and seldom conduct business in any way resembling the overground press. Thus most underground newspapers have a lifespan of approximately twelve to eighteen months if they attempt weekly publication.

Financing an underground newspaper is, at best, precarious. In August 1968, the Underground Press Syndicate asked its 79-paper membership, "Are You Making A Profit?" Only 28 per cent replied they were; 72 per cent were breaking even or losing money.

Most underground editors prefer promoting the goals of the radical political movement to paying their telephone or printing bills, so they publish pretty much on a week-to-week basis.

If an underground editor seeks longevity for his publication, he looks to the business and marketing blueprints of the Berkeley *Barb*, the *East Village Other*, the Los Angeles *Free Press*, or any financially successful overground newspaper. Most editors, however, prefer to "do their own thing" which is usually to be economically unsound and editorially free—as long as they have the money *up front.*

8 / Editorial Content

What's in It

*In truth, from one issue to the next, the only thing that
can be safely predicted is surprise.*

—*Avant-Garde Magazine*[1]

A NEWSPAPER IS, IN THE FINAL ANALYSIS, ITS OWN
vision of the world. The underground press in modern America
has been the youthful voice of rebellion and joy struggling with
its own changing vision of itself and the world. In its early days
it was a flower child sometimes almost wildly messianic. Then
it vacillated from frustrated, passionate, and venomous attacks on
the establishment to meditation and withdrawal into astrology,
poetry, prophesy, and dreams of rural utopias. It moved in cycles as did its mobile, youthful audience and against what Bob
Rudnick of *EVO* claimed to be the "diarrhetic hate and scare
mongering that predominates in the official (American) press."[2]
Throughout the short history of the underground press, its vision
often appears to be of another world altogether.

Where the establishment press has Richard Nixon, Spiro T.
Agnew, and Billy Graham, the underground papers have Tom Hayden, Eldridge Cleaver, and Kirby T. Hensley. The establishment
press makes folk heroes out of Dean Martin, Twiggy, and the

astronauts. The underground press does the same for Tim Leary, Allen Ginsberg, and Che Guevara. The overground makes oracles of George Washington, J. Edgar Hoover, and General Westmoreland, while the underground praises Marx, Malcolm X and Marshall McLuhan. Establishment papers cover weddings, deaths, sporting events, and the stock market, while the underground concentrates on radical politics, psychedelic drugs, and religious prophecy. The establishment press fights communism, hippies, free-love, narcotics, and sexual deviations while the underground battles the police, the CIA, the university administrations, and any other spokesman for the American establishment.

The growing underground audience can best be described as young or wanting to be young and opposed to the social status quo as viewed by the establishment press. But even among the underground press itself, there is a wide split between the radically political papers and the radically cultural papers.

Defined simply, the political papers emphasize radical politics and believe the underground press should be used as tools for a political revolution. The cultural papers, on the other hand, are interested in the total complex of relations between all people in the movement and work toward a general awareness in American society.

The political papers are represented by the *Guardian* and the *Rat* in New York City, the *Free Presses* in Washington and in Philadelphia, *The Old Mole* in Cambridge, *The Black Panther* and *The Movement* in the Bay Area, and the SDS-aligned Liberation News Service, which provides much of the national political view for all of them. Underground papers more concerned with a cultural view of American society are often as radically opposed to the system but include news and writing dealing with matters other than radical politics. Among the major cultural sheets are the *East Village Other, Barb, The Seed, Kaleidoscope, The Realist, Other Scenes, Rolling Stone,* the now commercial San Francisco *Oracle* and the Underground Press Syndicate which provides the action center for such papers.

The content in both political and cultural underground papers differs most from that of their overground brothers in their view of the importance of 1) objectivity, 2) balanced reporting, and 3) advertising. Advertising in the underground press is, as noted above, just about the reverse of the 65 per cent advertising to 35 per cent nonadvertising content ratio in the establishment press.

Subjectivity is a journalistic principle among underground press staffers and they care much more about opinion than fact. A sign in the Berkeley *Barb* office, "Put down prejudice—unless it's on our side," best describes subjective reporting and, also, why the "objectivity" standard of the establishment press is rejected. Objectivity is assumed to imply a lack of involvement with the subject, and noninvolvement is a cardinal underground sin—particularly on radically political staffs. Being involved in the action and being opposed to the establishment is a formula for an exciting brand of personal journalism, even if it presents only one side of the story. Underground journalists believe readers can get all the "law and order" viewpoint they want from the daily press, and reporters see themselves first as activists and only incidentally as journalists. Here is an example of such personal-involvement reporting from Stew Albert in the Berkeley *Barb*, a day before the People's Park incident:

> People's Park may be a Pigs' Pen by the time you read this, Roger Heyns has proclaimed his eternal loyalty to cement and soccer and his game begins with the motor of a bulldozer and the barrel of a mad pig's gun.
>
> The creators of our Park wanted nothing more than to extend their spirits into a gracious green meandering plaything. They wanted to make beauty more than an empty word in a spray net commercial.
>
> Our Park has been the greatest success in the history of New Berkeley. Thousands of sisters and brothers poured their flesh and sweat into the Roger Heyns parking lot swamp and in an unfolding sod raised work to the level of art.
>
> Each morning children come smiling into their Park and are

instant equals. The People's Park is everybody's childhood daydream—the big rock candy mountain in back of Telegraph Avenue.

On Wednesday the people of the Park met in a planned-to-be but still dry fish pond. The majority were longhairs of the street and university farmer-artists out to save their land. They had word Roger Heyns was going to build a Berlin wall around their dream.[3]

or Mike Hodel on radio reporting in *Open City*:

Dial-diddling in Los Angeles radio can result in a plethora of pessimism and the feeling that your ears may be drowned in a torrent of stupidity. But once in a while, your attention can be caught and concentrated on a few flowers amid the mud.[4]

And Sheila Golden reporting on a Black Panther trial in *Other Scenes*:

The scene of the action was the New York Criminal Court Building at 100 Center Street, where less than three weeks before over a thousand outraged students and members of the black community demonstrated against the jailing of 21 Black Panthers.

This time it was lawyers themselves on the picket line protesting not only the nationwide campaign to destroy the Black Panther Party, but also the perversion of the legal system generally.

The theme of the demonstration, carried on simultaneously by more than a 100 law students in front of the U.S. Courthouse and New York Supreme Court in nearby Foley Square was "Confront the Courts for Criminal Justice."[5]

None of the underground writers accept the role of detached observer since that would eliminate the element of involvement so necessary to the new left's self-identity.

If the underground press in any way mirrors a segment of disaffected American youth, that mirror reflects more than just acrid political opposition. The *Los Angeles Free Press* features a wide-ranging view of Los Angeles' hip community. Breaking the content down into news, editorials, features, comics, art, and advertising, the *Freep* allocated 11 per cent of its space to news reporting, 19 per cent to features, 12 per cent to art, 2 per cent to editorial comment, and 45 per cent to advertising. The remaining 11 per cent was inconsistently allotted to comics, poetry, a calendar of events, and promotions. These figures are based on a study of eight consecutive issues in 1967.[6]

A quick look at the now defunct *Open City* and *Los Angeles Oracle* indicate why *Freep* carried so little art and poetry and so much advertising. Over eight issues, *Oracle* and *Open City* gave 18 and 22 per cent to advertising, 41 and 22 per cent to art, 30 and 27 per cent to features and 3 and 9 per cent to news. *Oracle* carried only 8 per cent of public service materials like a community calendar or classified ads, while *Open City* ran nearly 20 per cent of such materials.[7]

Comparisons are as odious with underground papers as other things, but the willingness of *Open City* and *Oracle* to satisfy the psychedelic fringe of Los Angeles' hip audience with color and freaked-out art was undoubtedly the reason *Freep* emphasized news and features. *Freep* considers itself an alternative to the *Los Angeles Times* and has a lot more coverage of city politics than most underground papers. After the Watts upheaval in 1965 *Freep* beat all overground media with a lengthy analysis of the reasons for unrest in that community. *Freep* features an exceptionally comprehensive coverage of Los Angeles theater, both underground and legitimate, and carries a monthly 24-page insert entitled "Living Arts" with contributors like Lawrence Lipton, John Carpenter, Jerry Hopkins and other well known California writers.

One of the most outstanding contributions of *Freep* to the West Coast subterranean scene are the political cartoons of Ron Cobb. Syndicated in many underground papers, Cobb draws ominous, dark sketches of America at the brink of destruction, showing dehumanization and death of the individual at the hands of technology and the bureaucratic establishment. (Plate 11)

East Village Other is a second cultural underground sheet that offers a wide and changing variety of subject matter to its readers. EVO's major distinction is the use of satirical comic strips, far-out classified ads, and bizarre poetry. Comic strips are as American as television or apple pie and were first introduced to American journalism in the late 1890s as circulation builders on newspapers. During the '30s the slapstick strips were eclipsed by storytelling panels concerned with the family, getting a job, and security. Where Establishment strips mirror the middleclass scene, EVO's comics feature sex, drugs, police brutality, and general taboo-breaking. EVO's contributions include Art Spiegelman's "Adventures of a Jolly Jack-Off, the Masturbation Fiend," Spain Rodriguez' "Trashman, Agent of the Underground Revolt," Kim Deitch's psychedelic Alice in Wonderland, "Sunshine Girl," and Bill Beskman's "Captain High," the superman defender who protects heads (drug users) from the fuzz.

Underground comics are evidence of the new media's willingness to satirize American society without taboos. They lean heavily on long hair, drugs, radical politics, sexual freedom, and anything else that will offend the establishment mentality and consequently please the underground reader. *East Village Other* was one of the first underground publications on the comics scene and there soon followed publications like *Yellow Dog*, "a nitty gritty dog pissing on the deepest symbol of American consciousness"; *Snatch Comics*, "a further assault on the American Dream"; and The *Gothic Blimp Works*, featuring such entries as "Mr. Know-it-all and his Pal Diz in *What The Fuck*." *Gothic Blimp Works* was the first underground, all color comix newspaper and was circulating 25,000 copies monthly after its first three issues early in 1969.

Ten 1969 issues of EVO devoted 46 per cent to advertising, 16 per cent to comix, 28 per cent to feature articles, 4 per cent to editorials, 2 per cent to calendars, and 4 per cent to news. Twelve per cent of the advertising space was used for the classifieds which were another *EVO* first in the underground press. *EVO*'s classified ads emphasize sexual freedom for all—heterosexual, homosexual, or combinations. Katzman believes his classified ads are neither obscene nor deviant, claiming "These ads help get people together. Before we started running *Wheel and Deal* (the overline on its three pages of unclassifiable classifieds) these people had no outlets for their sexual interests. Now they're getting together and there is less loneliness in New York City." Classified advertising copy in *EVO*[8] usually reads:

> *Calling all women from 18 to 30. Let a man of 24 share the pleasures sex has to offer to one another. Call—— between 5 and 9 p.m. Ask for Barry.*

or

> *The new fad!! Color your pubic hair any shade you wish! Green, red, bright orange, light blonde or magenta! Surprise your friends. The next time your crowd gets together for a party, be known as 'the girl with the green pussy' or 'the fellow with the pink peter.' Send $5.00 today to——.*

or

> *Discreet, groovy guy, early 30's, handsome, hung and horny! Looking for similar males for uninhibited mutual delight in twosomes or threesomes! Send details and photo if possible to——.*

Paul Krassner of the *Realist* claims sexual freedom is a political thing since it involves a person's freedom to do what he or she wants with his or her body. Whatever the political implications, many underground newspapers have been sued, harassed, and even closed down by means of the obscenity laws in certain state and regional jurisdictions, and the United States Post Office authorities have disrupted mail distribution on the same grounds. Many politically inclined publications avoid obscenity simply because they want to arouse the establishment on more political issues.

A wide range of features and self-help columns set the cultural papers apart from their more politically-oriented counterparts. A column in John Wilcock's *Other Scenes* called "Phoney Facts" explained in detail how to "diddle" the telephone company. It read: "Install your own extension phones and save the rent of a Princess; for long-distance calls, record lengthy messages and play them into the mouthpiece at high speed to be decoded at the other end at normal speed."[9]

One of the most popular columns in the Los Angeles *Freep* and fifteen other cultural and radical underground publications is Dr. HIPPOCRATES. The good Dr. Hip is Eugene Schoenfeld, M.D., a Berkeley medical-treatment-for-pay drop-out, whose column specializes in the treatment of aberrant sexual behavior. A sort of "Dear Abby" for the hip set, Dr. Hippocrates answers questions on sex, drugs, and other non-conforming habits unlikely to be answered by the overground press' Dr. Crane. Dr. Hip answers them thoughtfully and often humorously. Typical questions are, Can pot or LSD be given safely to children, puppy dogs, or cats? Is it harmful to fart in the presence of others? Should a bent penis be straightened? Is masturbation harmful to one's eyesight? Here are a few exchanges typical with Dr. Hippocrates:

Question: *In the showers I notice all very fat men have a penis barely an inch long. Why?*

Answer: *An aroused (angered) colleague stoutly maintains this is a false observation, caused, no doubt, by lack of familiarity with obese people. Increased fat tissues covering the base of the penis accounts for this belief. Have you ever read about Fatty Arbuckle?*

Question: *Is masturbation physically harmful if I do it once a day?*

Answer: *There is a story about a little boy who was found masturbating and told that he would go blind unless he stopped. "Well," he pleaded, "can I do it until I need eyeglasses?" There is no evidence that masturbation is physically or mentally harmful whatever its frequency.*

Question: *I have been getting a rather weird high by smoking a tobacco cigarette like a joint. A drag will start me up and two cigarettes will get me totally zonked. I usually don't smoke (except grass). Do you have any idea about the medical ramifications of this habit?*

Answer: *Cigarettes are a known health hazard. Do you get them from The Friendly Stranger?*

Question: *I have a 'condition' which seems to worry my husband more than myself. Ever since my teens my inner or minor vaginal lips have hung outside my major lips. Because they are not neatly within my major lips my husband believes this could indicate some disorder. What do you think?*

Answer: *There is nothing abnormal about the labia minora protruding through the labia majora. Why, some of my best friends. . . .*[10]

Dr. Hip originated in the Berkeley *Barb* and is now syndicated in fifteen underground papers. Many other underground papers pick up Dr. Hippocrates without bothering to pay when the column carries questions that interest their editors. By August 1969, the overground San Francisco Sunday *Chronicle* had picked up his column as a regular feature. Anonymous features are used widely in the underground because of the pressure put on staffers by police and narcotics agents. Along with many articles credited to the fictitious Intergalactic World Brain, the *Barb* features Sergeant Pepper's column on Vietnam and the mysterious Roving Rat Fink, a column of opinions on everything under the political and cultural sun. Sometimes entire underground staffs use aliases or put-on names to avoid being identified. Columns by Lenny the Lewd, the Grass Prophet, or William Randolph Hearst are sometimes cover-ups, sometimes put-ons, with the actual writers usually well-known to staffers and readers alike.

Another popular feature in the cultural papers is a weekly astrology guide. When radical politics became hip in 1967, many of the political papers swung away from Astrology, but it remained a mainstay in *Great Speckled Bird, Helix,* and *Kaleidoscope.* Entitled "the Gigantic Tent of Hermes Trismegistics," "The Aquarian Age," or simply "Using Astrology," the feature was carried as the religious prophesy of the movement. Astrology preached the unification of religions, science, and technology, and many of the NOW children of the underground audience followed it as their weekly bread.

Underground readers are not the only readers who approve of underground style or content. Joan Didion in *The Saturday Evening Post* called the underground press: "Strident and brash, but they do not irritate; they have the faults of a friend, not of a monolith." Miss Didion concluded: "They are the only American newspapers that do not leave me in the grip of a profound physical conviction that the oxygen has been cut off from my brain tissue."[11] *Look* magazine noted in an article: "What's happened is not the point (of the underground press), 'What's happening' is."[12]

Less complimentary was the following statement from *American Opinion*, the official organ of the John Birch Society:

> The editorial format of the underground press calls for a Marxist message blanketed in sex and drugs. This is kneaded with four-letter words, malapropped with polysyllables, and stirred with corny revolutionary slogans that would have embarrassed an East Side anarchist of 1910. It is mixed with 'hip' language taken from the lexicons of Marx, Lenin and Chairman Mao, along with the weird vernacular of the Hindu mystics. Served with a quart of self-righteousness, the above recipe produces the nicest little revolutionary stew you ever saw.[13]

The underground press unquestionably deals with Hindu mystics, Marx, Lenin, and Chairman Mao. They also include sex, jazz, and narcotics, since that's what their editors and readers are interested in.

When asked what the underground press cared about, Tom Forcade of the Underground Press Syndicate wrote in *Orpheus*:

*Radical theater, sexual freedom, the taboo against knowing
who you are, communes, anarchy, draft resistance, light shows,
peace and freedom, hashish and a thousand other things and
non-things, real and imagined, ridiculous and sublime.*[14]

Since their doings are largely ignored by the overground press,
most movement members find their calendar of events on underground pages. Such calendars feature a listing of where it's going
to be at on the hip scene for the coming week. Titled "Scendrome,"
"Happenings," or "Trips—Free and Not-So-Free" (many events
are free to members of the movement) these announcements serve
as social guidelines for activists and cultural hipsters alike and are
followed religiously by the turned-on generation.

Coverage of musical groups, individuals, and concerts takes up
much of the feature space of the papers. Electronically-controlled
rock music as an intensely participational, non-linear art form has
become the sound of revolution and, as such, a bridge between
politically and culturally oriented papers. *Rolling Stone* in San
Francisco is dedicated almost solely to the rock music scene and
is a must for advertisers of rock albums. *Rolling Stone's* eleven-page
analysis of Groupies, the male and female sleep-in followers of rock
musicians, in a February 1969 issue was an outstanding example of
what the underground press can do with in-depth reporting.[15] *Distant Drummer* is, and the now-defunct *Open City* was, largely concerned with the rock music world, with stories about individual
performers as well as reviews of groups popular among the underground audience.

When reviews of rock music are included in the *Movement,
Guardian,* or other politically-oriented new left papers, they are
usually selected, analyzed, and judged according to their political
value to the movement. The political sheets are more interested in
the protest songs of Bob Dylan and Phil Ochs than the grinding,
hipswiveling sounds of Jimmy Hendrix or Janis Joplin.

Establishment media in general are another target of the alternative press, which takes strong issue with the establishment's definition of news. The following analysis by Marty Glass in *Dock of the Bay*'s third issue in August 1969, speaks powerfully about how the underground defines news:

> There's been a lot of murder and rape in the Bay Area during the past few weeks.
>
> A pregnant woman was raped and stabbed in the throat with a butcher knife by two men in the Haight. Two San Jose girls, 14 & 15, were discovered with hundreds of stab wounds in their bodies. A 17-year old girl from Salinas found strangled with a red belt; police suspect this job was linked with the murder of eight girls in Ann Arbor, Michigan. A gang attack in the Hunter's Point section of San Francisco led to one man murdered, his girl raped, and his father slashed. And then there's the weird L.A. movie star murders of Sharon Tate, the pregnant wife of Roman Polanski, and three friends in their secluded Bel Air mansion.
>
> There have been 96 murders so far this year in the Bay Area, just six less than the total for 1968.
>
> The Bay Area newspapers blazed out the news in giant headlines. "Savage Slaying Mystery," "Shocking Murder," "A Story of Savagery," "Big Search for Knife Killer of Two San Jose Girls," "Big Hunt for Picnic Killer," and so on.
>
> There's a big lie behind all this. The stories are more or less true; the accounts bear some police-filtered relation to the truth, but there's still a big lie behind the grisly intimate details of bloody mayhem and brutal sexual assault.
>
> The lie is linked to the idea of 'news' in the daily papers. What does 'news' mean? 'News' is what stands out on the vast, flat and presumably irrelevant plain of mundane events, 'news' is what deviates from the ordinary and the normal, 'news' is what someone else decides is important.
>
> Supposedly, everything which isn't worth knowing about isn't of public concern. The daily papers convey a very strong and very indirect message; there's a normal, everyday life which is OK and unexceptional—not worth talking about. And then

there's 'news': anything which stands out, anything that doesn't happen all the time and is, therefore, of interest.

Life is good. That's the realm where things are taken care of. 'News' is when something goes wrong.

This is pure bullshit. The real news isn't in distinct, bizarre events. The real news is what happens 24 hours a day all day long everywhere. This is the news we don't read about in the daily papers because the people who control those papers don't want us to know about it and do everything they can to distract our attention from it.

Fortunately, they can't succeed. We don't need their papers to tell us about the real news. All we have to do is open our eyes.

The real news is the expression on the faces of children sitting in tenement doorways with nothing to do. The real news is the tenement itself.

The real news is the despair and humiliation on the faces of people waiting for hours for a lousy check in the welfare or unemployment offices. And it's also on the emptied faces of people who have jobs they hate, jobs where their creative potential is stifled and crushed under the weight of meaningless labor performed to make enough money to survive.

The real news is jobs created solely to provide profits for those who don't work at all, or for a corporation which is nothing but a bankbook.

The precious unredeemable time of our lives is sacrificed for numbers in bankbooks.

The real news is elderly people rotting away in dilapidated Old Folks' Homes or in spare rooms in their childrens' houses, unwanted, resented, feeling they might as well be dead. The real news is in the millions of people who don't get enough to eat, who receive inadequate medical care, who suffer and die from diseases which could be cured and should never have been contracted in the first place.

The reals news is when there's a giant traffic jam on the Bay Bridge because the market economy and capitalism require profit and there's no profit in safe, comfortable, efficient, rapid public transportation. The real news is that there are hardly enough parks and playgrounds for a fraction of our children, that schools are falling apart, overcrowded, repressive, irrelevant and hated by the children imprisoned there.

The real news is that guys are getting beaten by sadistic psychopaths in prisons and army stockades all over the country, kids watch hours of obscene commercials on TV, women are forced to waste their lives in shopping and cooking because private consumption is the syphilitic deity of our society.

The real news is that people who can't take it any more—and they're mostly black or poor whites—are called mentally ill and given shock treatment or mind-killing drugs.

The real news is that ten thousand women die every year in the United States from slipshod expensive abortions, because this system doesn't permit half the population to decide what goes on in their own bodies, doesn't provide for any way outside of the decayed institution of marriage for children to be cared for.

The real news is that cops who murder black men are given medals and a guy found with two joints gets ten years.

The real news is that guys are being forced to kill their brothers in Vietnam.

The real news is that all the important decisions made in this country are made by maniac insects with dollar signs engraved on their beady inhuman plastic eyeballs. We see their pictures every day on the business pages in their newspapers.

The real news is that Huey Newton is in jail and Richard Nixon isn't. . . .[16]

This dramatic statement by Glass on what is and what is not news comes close to clarifying many of the differences between over- and underground publications.

Another characteristic of underground newspaper makeup is front-page photos, art, and illustrations around a single incident. The *East Village Other* photo of President Johnson's head grafted onto the body of a Nazi storm trooper has been mentioned; the *Movement* once ran a reverse line art drawing of a black fist, symbol of Afro-American demands for equality; and half-tone shots of female nudes, militant leaders, or underground oracles are common fare for the new media's covers. Because of liberal use of white space, flexibility in using colored newsprint, and a willingness to experiment with photos, type, and art work, underground front pages resemble magazine covers more than overground tabloid newspapers.

Athletics are largely ignored by underground editors, although *Seed* and *Good Times* ran irregular satirical columns on sports for a time.

Obituaries are another feature glaringly absent in the dissenting press, an omission undoubtedly related to the hippie subculture's mystical attitude towards death. Dropping out or withdrawing from society symbolizes their own death and the so-called enlightenment that comes from drugs is considered a rebirth. Thus obituaries are generally restricted to those of an office cat or someone's stray dog.

Poetry is a popular feature in many of the culturally-inclined underground papers. The poetic themes ordinarily concern movement events, psychedelic experiences, or the beauties of nature.

Liberation News Service and the Underground Press Syndicate are an extension of the political and cultural underground press, and their differences best explain the split within the medium. Strongly oriented to the politics of revolution, LNS spends most of its time gathering and disseminating news and information of a radical political nature. Bloody confrontations between students, police and college administrators are higher on LNS's value scale than psychedelic art, rock music, or drugs. LNS claims to feature "humorous art work, satirical poetry and cultural material" but a scanning of several dozen LNS packets revealed precious little to substantiate such claims. More characteristic of this somewhat humorless service are articles on "the Christian Anti-Communist Crusade," the "Revolutionary Youth Movement," "Congress Investigation of SDS," or "Berkeley—Life with National Guards."[17]

The Underground Press Syndicate identifies more strongly with the cultural papers although it makes its services available to any and all underground papers and maintains a cooperative relationship with LNS. Seriously concerned with the future of films and broadcasting, UPS covers a wider variety of underground activities than just radical or revolutionary politics.

The underground split between radical activists and nonpolitical drop-outs is in many ways a division into different cultural aspects of the same youth movement. There are powerful forces determining the quality of American life both under- and overground and it is unlikely to be improved singlehandedly by any centralization of effort on politics, culture, music, or satire. Unless the LNS and radically political papers in the underground press realize there is more to the cultural revolution than revolutionary confrontation politics, they will fall into the limbo of other American special interest publications. The cultural papers have kept at least one foot in the broader youth movement bag and in that bag there is a variety of content and life as wide as the future of American youth—over- or underground.

9 / Language Analysis

How It's Written

The air of this time and place is so heavy with rhetoric,
so thick with soothing lies, that one must really do
great violence to language, one must somehow
disrupt the comforting beat, in order to be heard.

—JAMES BALDWIN[1]

BOB DYLAN WROTE "THE TIMES THEY ARE A-Changin'" in 1966, and by 1968 Ralph Gleason, rock music critic for the *San Francisco Chronicle*, observed: "The language she is changing," too.[2] By 1970 the times and the language had indeed changed and the changes seemed to parallel the development of the new medium.

For the preceding generation to be "square" was to be·dependable. "Cool," "Crazy," and "Real Neat," followed in succession as American youth sought fresh, inoffensive ways to express themselves as they began their climb up the economic ladder. Many, many things happened to America in the 60s to change escapism to involvement and this involvement brought about a whole new language for the age. The underground press sought words to express experiences for which words did not exist, used words to mock and satirize the Establishment and adapted the street lingo of American ghettoes as an expression of individuality. It was inevitable that the new language should find its expression in the

113

underground press since it was the only medium turned-on to the "involved" generation.[3]

Something can be learned about the underground press by simply examining the manner in which the papers are named. Fresh, crazy, biased, irreverent, "camp," and often unexpectedly inventive, the directors of the new media do not ordinarily settle for traditional nomenclature like the *Times*, the *Tribune*, or the *Clarion* (unless, of course, they can in some way tease, mock, or put-on the establishment press by such titles). The *Daily Meadow Muffin*, *Raisin Bread*, and the *79¢ Spread* are not things to eat but names of papers in New York City, Minneapolis, and Monterey. *Mother of Voices*, *Hard Times*, and *Love Street* are other publications in New York City, Washington, and San Francisco, so christened because of the staff's opposition to the establishment, the absurdity of the world as they see it, or the title's appropriateness to the publication and the times. Bizarre titles like *News From Nowhere*, the *New York Roach*, and the *Wretched Mess News* were bestowed in Illinois, New York, and Montana, to demonstrate that the editors refused to take their publications too seriously. The inventiveness in the titles of the new papers appears endless: *Paper Highway*, *Paper Tiger*, *Paper Bag*, the *Rat*, the *Rag*, *Greenfeel*, *Bullsheet*, *Bandersnatch*, and the highly irreverent *Yellow Dog*, the paper that pisses on the American establishment. Others come on with *Teaspoon Door*, *Mega Middle Myth*, *Georgia Straight*, *Spokane Natural*, *Marshmallow*, *Screw*, *Walrus*, *Hinky Dinky Report*, *Hair*, *Sons of Jabberwock*, *Pith*, *Non-Paper*, *Loving Couch Press*, *Intercourse*, *Brief Candle*, *Crocodile*, *Crawdaddy*, *Great Speckled Bird*, *Left Out*, *Octopus*, *Salty Dog*, *Ungarbled Word*, and on and on.

In the 1950s no such papers existed and obscenity was considered to reside exclusively in a deprived, frustrated American underbelly. Moreover, use of it was looked upon as unacceptable to the upwardly mobile young middle class. The concept of open use of gut and gutter language as being indicative of class disappeared quickly as the 50s faded into the 60s. Drugs, rock music, and D. H.

Lawrence helped define the new language of involvement, and the underground press served as the arteries through which the new mode of expression flowed. Such expression became highly personal, emotional, and irreverent, very much like the life style of the rough house, ghetto class with whom it joined hands.

The audience of underground newspapers began to advertise openly for everything from group orgies to LSD formulae to French Ticklers. The personal ads in the classified began to read, "Orgy guide: Get some flesh! Sex-filled . . . places to go in LA."[4] The new language was slanted against puritanical sex attitudes, the war in Vietnam, and the American Establishment; and it was for, as the saying went, "Peace, Pussy, and Pot." Gutter language became gut journalism and the new expression found its voice in the first columns of the experimental press.

D. H. Lawrence introduced a new form of sexual and emotional freedom with his direct use of language in *Lady Chatterley's Lover,* tame as that 1928 work may seem now. In it gamekeeper Mellors was presented as a splendid specimen of manhood, whereas Chatterley had been sexually crippled and was immobilized in a wheelchair—an obvious symbol of the middle class's emotional paralysis and impotence. Over a million copies of the book were sold[5] during revival of interest in the book in the 50s and it became very *in* to be vocal and descriptive about sex. Middle-class students in Berkeley were carrying four-letter signs demanding free speech, and the language revolution was underway. To refer casually to a university administrator or any established authority figure as "an uptight motherfucker" became a symbol of the hip culture. One of the most striking aspects of contemporary gut language is that men and women alike use it without the slightest sign of embarrassment. When a smiling woman demonstrator with the sign "Every Woman Secretly Wants To Be RAPED" was pictured on the front page of the *San Francisco Express-Times,* nobody blinked an eye.[6]

Television was undoubtedly instrumental in the breakdown of the fragmented, specialized world of the 1950s. "Interdependency" was a big word in the college classrooms of the 60s as television tended to bring the world together as a McLuhanesque global village. Much of the all-at-onceness of young people "turned on," "tuned in," or "dropped out" was a creation of the electronic age, and the new style in language was merely an expression of that total experience. Television gave American youth a sense of being "in the world" of immediate gratification while many religious institutions argued that the important world was over the horizon in the future. Thus terms such as "copped out," "dropped out," and "split," were introduced by a generation of runaways who refused to live by institutionalized behavioral standards. The generation discovered McLuhan and saw their parents driving down the road looking in the rearview mirror in a Bonanzaland stage coach. "Square" became repugnant and "cool" became a symbol of acceptance as the new generation changed the meaning of old words and put new and old together in an effort to express their sought-after or new-found individuality. "Sock It To Me" on television's "Laugh-In" with its sexual overtones had traveled some distance from its original meaning as little old ladies or television nuns were casually imploring TV comedians to "Sock It To Me." The sales "rebellions" of automobile campaigns and the "Whatever Turns You On" expression of the TV comics reflected a revolution in language brought about in part by the television medium itself.

The term "your aunt" came to mean an older homosexual who wanted to take care of a younger man, while the change in connotation of the word "mother" signalled a breakdown, or at least a shift, in the meaning of family according to the rapidly-changing dictionary of the young.

It was perhaps the introduction of psychedelic drugs, more than any other single agent, that turned the electronic TV generation on to themselves. Paul Krassner told his *Mad Magazine* graduates in the *Realist* that "autonomy is power" which he suggested they get from "Blake, or however you first got laid, or the precipitating chemicals—pot, grass, or LSD." The *Realist* quoted Confucius as having said: "To straighten out the nation, straighten the provinces; to straighten the province, straighten the city; to straighten the city, straighten households; to straighten your household, straighten your family, straighten yourself."[7] Dylan told his audiences to "Dig yourselves," a missionary group in San Francisco's Haight-Ashbury district published the "Digger Papers" while underground newspapers emphasizing radical politics asked their readers about the revolution: "Can you Dig It?" "Dig" meant to probe, search, or understand and when hip people understood one another they nodded with "I dig." The new language reprimanded the establishment for being "straight" while lauding its users for getting their heads "straight." Language needed no reference and the message became clear by the feeling in the voice or by the way it was enunciated. Feeling displaced logic and thus the intense personal report replaced the so-called logical, balanced journalism of the establishment press.

Much of the writing in the underground press is termed psychedelic and resounds with the "tripping out" hallucinogenic experiences of drug users. EVO's Bob Rudnick writing on the "Fifth Estate" takes off on the Establishment press, and the following account is more like a run-on drug experience than a news story:

> ... What whore American integrity, the fourth estate is not merely licking the cracks of the advertisers but burying its head in a wave of paranoia directly extracted (not even original) from the Big Brother (I pledge allegiance) literature through the vocal diarrhetic hate and scare mongering that predominates official press super government WE-they releases. The slave dead-think regular media reprint the whitewash bullshit, manytimes lies of the fascist managed, distorted bullshit as fact, without comment or even checking for truth with the utter disregard and contempt either for their mob-crazed, America first puppet readers or the few naive believers in the check and balance system of a fourth estate on the government, the aristocratic, imperialistic dollar pimps. The popular media are merely electronic propaganda outlets for a diabolical psychotic society's phony government which attempts a total faceless no thought populace without the right even to question much

less dissent or even oppose. The current trend rivals the most
effective fascist and totalitarian communist regime in its
suppressive spectre, to coalesce into the conforming
grey morass.[8]

The pattern-breaking effect of drugs created much of the new, turned-on verbiage, and the release from old verbal inhibitions resulted from "tripping out" on drugs. As the grandparents of today's hippies got their kicks from illegal bathtub gin and smuggled whiskey, the youngsters get theirs from pot, speed, and LSD. Drugs were considered a catalyst to self-awareness by the drug culture, which soon discovered its own mode of speaking. The use of such language also grew because of the need for secrecy, since drugs were illegal. "Acid" was an hallucinogenic drug, a "bummer trip" was the nightmarish effect of a bad drug experience, and "freaking out" meant to lose control through the use of drugs. A "bag man" was a drug distributor, "a pusher" was the middle man, and a "head" was a steady user of LSD. "Narc," "Pot," and "grass" originated with the drug set, as did "lid," "joint," and "speed."

Calculated to put down as well as close out or reject parents, much of the hip culture language was a reaction to parents who were considered delinquent rather than permissive by their offspring. The rejection inherent in leaving a baby sitter to mind the kids while the parents frolicked night after night at the country club came back to haunt the parents. Their children designed a language to exclude them.

The now generation was raised on rock and roll music, and the central focus of underground journalism in the late 60s was the personal-involved-kind of hypertensive style that flows from that music. Chester Anderson wrote in one of the first San Francisco *Oracles* that "Rock is essentially head music and encompasses a vast potential for growth, development, adaptation and experimentation."[9] Many of the rock groups are intimately related, living communally and more closely than many American families. Because the music is highly participatory, the new medium answered a need created by the depersonalized, organized, established world. The fact that rock music is largely non-typographic explains much of the underground press's emphasis on line art, psychedelic drawings, photographic essays, and wild colors. It also explains partially why underground newspapers carry so little news as it is generally defined in journalism textbooks. Even the term "type-head," used first by the Berkeley *Barb* to justify the presence of so many news stories in one issue, spun off from the drug term "acid head." The group participation of listening to the Jefferson Airplane, the Grateful Dead, or Country Joe and the Fish became a very tribal experience. The message of the new artists was feeling not thinking, and the words of Bob Dylan expressed those feelings in poetry. Dylan was the first to urge American youth to "dig yourself," to implore American adults "To admit that the waters around them had grown," and to remind the establishment "that the times they are a-changin'."

There is a whole glossary of terms emanating from the soul and rock music scene and many of the words were first introduced by the underground press.

A willingness to express feeling along with content and a tendency to use obscenity as a shock tactic to awaken an insensitive monolithic adult society have been characteristic of the underground press's assault on the establishment's language bank. United States Supreme Court rulings in the mid-60s making language acceptable as long as it had "redeeming social values," gave the underground press impetus in its push for "totally free expression."

So if you have "hang-ups," are "uptight," are in your own "bag," or just feel "groovy," attribute it to the underground press. They printed much of it first and will undoubtedly continue to offer an outlet for the expression of gut language in the 1970s.

* * *

A glossary of terms used in the underground press is included at the end of the book beginning on page 175.

Who Reads It

Who is the underground?
You are, if you think, dream and work towards
the improvements and changes in your life,
towards the expectations for a better existence. . . .

—Boston *Avatar*[1]

ONE OF THE MOST DIFFICULT PROBLEMS IN ANA-
lyzing the underground press is to determine just how many and
which people read the product. In 1968 *The Wall Street Journal*
claimed an "estimated third of a million" read the underground
press,[2] *Newsweek* claimed a total underground circulation of 2-
million,[3] and the *Nation* quoted Marshall Bloom, then of Liberation News Service as estimating readership at 4.6-million,[4] while
the Underground Press Syndicate claimed 30-million readers. UPS
makes a distinction between the number of papers circulated and
the number of readers. They believe an average of six persons reads
each of the claimed 5-million copies sold, but complain that "170-
million Americans are not yet reached." UPS cited articles from
LNS, the Berkeley *Barb*, the *Guardian*, and the *Los Angeles Free
Press* that have been carried by many underground papers as further proof of the potential underground writing has for picking up
multiple readings. The claimed multiple readership of each paper
is attributed to the intensity of the content in underground papers

by UPS, whose coordinator, Tom Forcade, argues "the numbers game of trying to determine how many people read your paper is just another irrelevant gauge put on the underground press by the establishment to keep advertisers from supporting us."

UPS' claim of six readers for each paper sold is no doubt optimistic. However, at least in college communities, in their living groups, apartment houses, and dormitories, one can be sure that any available underground paper is perused by a lot more than one person. So whether there are one-third million or 30-million readers of underground papers in the United States may not be as significant as who those readers are.

Although formal studies of its readership are highly uncharacteristic of the informal underground press, *East Village Other* did conduct one such survey on 1,200 of its 65,000 subscribers. For whatever the results are worth, "71 per cent had attended college, 13 per cent had gone on to graduate school, 98 per cent had tried marijuana and 77 per cent had tried LSD."[5]

Underground newspapers reach an audience far wider than students and drug takers. Many elements of the Establishment who are interested in or sympathetic to the underground youth movement read the papers, as do tourists and those who seek partners for unusual sexual activities.

A reporter for the slapdash Berkeley *Barb* declared his readers were "fresh-smelling hippies and dewey-eyed runaways; potsmokers and pill poppers; university students and regents; socialists, Communists, anarchists and Yippies; draft resisters, black militants grape strikers, and community organizers; Hell's Angels, police chiefs, Indian chiefs, city councilmen, the Pentagon, and the Bank of America; moviegoers and record buyers; photographers and nudists; well-hung bi-guys, sadists, masochists, other assorted perverts and fetishists; a record number of venereal disease sufferers, and a scattering of journalists and tourists."[6]

Realist editor Paul Krassner lunched across from four elderly schoolteacher types in a New York East Side health food restaurant and, as he got up to leave, one lady asked him for his

"*Realist*-ic opinion of the New York City elections." Do elderly schoolteachers then read Krassner's bold, irreverent *Realist?* Maybe so, or maybe they recognized Krassner from the television programs on which he has appeared. The point is that many different elements of a community read underground papers.

Jesse Kornbluth wrote in his *Notes From the New Underground,* "Quite simply, an underground paper is generally written by the alienated for the alienated."[7] Those included in Kornbluth's alienated class are hippies, political activists, Latins, blacks, Chicanos, homosexuals, university and city drop-outs, or anyone in that large category known as "street people."

The thirty major papers included in this study represent most of the large circulation underground papers in the country. In New York City, however, the four pornographic sheets, *Kiss, Screw, Pleasure,* and *New York Review of Sex* were collectively printing over 350,000 in the summer of 1969. Paul Krassner of the *Realist* considers that a person's freedom to do what he chooses with his body is political. In this context the ground that these four publications are under is that of the puritan ethic and thus they may be classified as underground papers. This special category also includes the four San Francisco publications that cater to tourists: *Haight/Ashbury Tribune, Maverick, Love Street,* and the San Francisco *Oracle;* they contain a combination of nudes, poetry, and poster-sized art that make them souvenirs for the visiting firemen from Anytown, U.S.A.

Competition for readers is keen in the underground. Critical of the *Barb's* audience, one competing San Francisco *Good Times* staffer said the *Good Times* did not cater to the "geriatric, onanistic trade of the *Barb*" but averred that *Good Times* readers were "fairly young and hairy." He claimed even the Bay Area police read *Good Times* "as a prestige or status thing." Different underground papers attract different segments of the underground audience. Those interested in pornography are more apt to read the Sexual Freedom League's *Intercourse, Horseshit* magazine, or the "porny papers" mentioned above.

On the other hand, those more interested in radical politics would look to the *Movement,* the *Guardian,* or *New Left Notes* nationally, or the *Philadelphia Free Press,* the *Rat,* or the *Washington Free Press,* regionally. Readers in the New York City area with an interest in new or old left interpretation of cultural and political events get the popular *Village Voice* or the *East Village Other,* while on the West Coast such types get the Los Angeles *Free Press.* Those interested in musical interpretations of underground reality read *Rolling Stones, Crawdaddy* Magazine, or *Distant Drummer.*

For underground information with an international flavor, readers subscribe to *Other Scenes* in New York City, the *Georgia Straight* from British Columbia, or the *International Times* from London.

Military, Chicano, Black Militant, ethnic, and campus papers all feature news and information tailored to their specialized audiences. An analysis of the content of any of these papers can readily establish the fabric of the audience, as well as the point of view of the editors.

Determining the total circulation of underground papers is a task replete with contradictions, snarls, and inaccuracies. By the time one underground paper has reached a circulation peak, another one starts in the same region to cut into the competitor's circulation or to displace the original publication altogether. Below is a list of thirty papers included in the study for this book; their claimed circulation is over one million.

Of course, some of these (like the defunct Los Angeles *Oracle*) may not still be publishing at this rate, but other like publications probably will have replaced them.

Only the *Village Voice* and the *Los Angeles Free Press* have circulations confirmed by the Audit Bureau of Circulation; the others listed are personal statements of the publishers regarding the numbers they print. When and where possible, the present writer had circulation figures verified by the printer.

The Ally	12,000	New Left Notes	12,000
Boston Avatar	40,000	Los Angeles Oracle	60,000
Berkeley Barb	85,000	Realist	150,000
Black Panther	85,000	Good Times	12,000
Counterpoint	10,000	Village Voice	130,000
East Village Other	65,000	Philadelphia Free Press	25,000
Fifth Estate	17,000	Movement	20,000
Guardian	32,000	Kaleidoscope	40,000
Helix	15,000	Seed	24,000
Great Speckled Bird	12,000	Long Beach Free Press	12,000
Los Angeles Free Press	95,000	Washington Free Press	25,000
Old Mole	12,000	Distant Drummer	12,000
Peninsula Observer	5,000		

The 456 underground newspapers listed in the back of this book include some that are obviously not very underground, others that are not oriented toward radical politics or culture, and still others that are as specialized as the *Black Panther* or SDS's *New Left Notes*. Military, high school, and peace papers stretch the list even further. Underground newspapers have a notoriously high mortality rate, with new publications appearing and disappearing whenever a group of young people feel the need to express themselves, or tire of expressing themselves, in print. The list is a compilation of lists from the Liberation News Service, the Underground Press Syndicate, an underground press directory published by William D. Lutz of Stevens Point, Wisconsin, a list of California underground papers gathered by University of California graduate student Paul Slater, plus this writer's own list of some 100 otherwise unlisted papers. Whatever the exact number of underground papers or readers, the reader should bear in mind that the modern underground press movement did not get fully underway until 1964.

Between 1965 and 1969 the *East Village Other* grew from 5,000 to 65,000, the Berkeley *Barb* climbed from 1,200 to 85,000, and the Los Angeles *Free Press* rose from 5,000 to 95,000. Whatever estimate is accepted, the circulation is all the more impressive when the reader considers the great odds against which the papers are published. Forcade wrote in *Orpheus:*

> . . . *Although these papers have been evicted from their offices and homes, harassed by the police, had their sellers arrested en masse, had their benefit parties raided, been bombed, burned, beaten, duped, framed and lost printer after printer, the underground press continues to increase in size and number.*[8]

Who reads the underground press? Boston *Avatar* wrote: "If you think, dream, work, and build toward the improvements and changes in your life, your social and personal environments, toward the expectations of the better existence . . . The person next to you on the street car, as he proceeds to be where he wishes to be and do what he wishes to do," such are the potential underground press readers.

Who reads the underground press? The *Avatar* concluded:

> *"Think—look around—maybe*
> *in a mirror—maybe inside. . . ."*[9]

11 / Underground on Campuses

A Challenge to Educators

*In the classroom we teach freedom, but the
organization is totalitarian. The kids learn
that when the values of freedom and order
conflict, freedom recedes.*

—IRA GLASSER
New York Civil Liberties Union[1]

In CONSECUTIVE ARTICLES ON THE UNDERGROUND
press published in the May–June 1969 issue of *Student Life Highlights*, high school and college journalism advisers urged school
administrators to ignore or oppress controversy if it appeared in
campus underground publications. Mary F. Byan, advisor to the
school newspaper at Cubberly High School in Palo Alto, California, wrote:

> *Experience has proved that it is both unwise and unnecessary
> to take issue with an underground publication when it appears.
> An air of indifference is more effective than according it status
> through feud and argument. Absence of disproportionate
> administrative attention and concern deprives the underground
> of the stimulus needed for survival, of the notoriety it so
> desperately seeks.*[2]

In the same issue, Merritt Christensen, Assistant Journalism professor at Minot State College in North Dakota, suggested: "An

easy solution to the dilemma of editorial opposition to school administration is simply not to permit the publication of controversial issues or student opinions." This writer's intolerance and reaction to administrators' unwillingness to deal with alternative means of communication has been a major catalyst in precipitating this book.

The revolt of students in American schools and colleges cannot be met by turning aside one's eyes or by throwing sand on the revolt. Police repression and tighter administrative controls have not worked well at Berkeley, at Columbia, or at Ohio's Kent State University. The students in today's high schools and colleges often have been educated at home by parents who are better educated than their teachers. Furthermore, these children have been taught by mass media with which the teacher finds himself in competition and by actual participation in political rallies, sit-ins, be-ins, love-ins, and demonstrations. To accept the new reality of this training is to accept the challenge of American education in the 1970s. To reject the challenge is to reject the students themselves. The evolution of the underground press on American campuses is largely a reaction to such rejection.

By 1970 underground newspapers had sprung up on or near college and high school campuses all across the country. Here are a few case histories of how and why they were born. The *Daily Collegian* at Wayne State University, Detroit, had been a traditional American college newspaper. In 1967, Arthur Johnson, a radical activist student, became editor and the paper was renamed *South End* in reference to a neighboring ghetto section on Detroit's south side. *South End* gradually adopted a policy of covering news of hippies, revolution, racism, and peace marches. During its two-year existence, the paper assumed a purely critical stance in evaluating the university in particular and the American society in general. The following editorial telling where Wayne State University was at typifies *South End's* tone:

> The university is bounded on the north by the central offices of the General Motors Corp., by far the wealthiest corporation in

*the world, an international symbol of the power of America
and the validity of American economic values. To the south of
the campus lies the Detroit black ghetto, scene of the two worst
race riots of the century, national symbol of the powerless and
the failure of American economic values.*

*And this university is caught in the pincer of this
contradiction.*[3]

South End continued along its revolutionary road until July 1969
when Wayne State President William R. Keast tried to suspend
the publication, announcing, "I am convinced that its [further]
publication would do serious damage to Wayne State University
and to the future of student journalism here." The student staff
led by John Watson, a black revolutionary, continued to publish
South End after the administrative threat with financing from
outside the university.

Equally worried about the future of journalism at Temple University, a group of graduate students started the *Temple Free Press*
in 1968. Opposed to what they considered the school of journalism's unwillingness to allow critical comment on the Vietnam
War and news about the radical political movement on campus,
the *Free Press* in eighteen months surpassed the University's *Temple News* in circulation and number of pages per issue. Circulating
25,000 copies, the *Free Press* changed its name to *Philadelphia
Free Press*, and was distributed free at nearby Bryn Mawr, Haver-
ford, Drexel, Swarthmore, and Philadelphia City Colleges. When
Pennsylvania State University's main campuses banned sales of
the *Free Press*, another college underground paper, the *Water
Tunnel State College Free Press*, increased its circulation to fill
the gap.

Print opposition to university administrations has cropped up
all over the country. In Lansing, Michigan, the *Paper* was in competition with the Michigan State College daily for four years until
summer 1969, when the staff decided to call it quits. Before the
Paper's demise, it carried a comic strip entitled "Land Grant Man"
in which the hero, President Palindrome of Midwestern Multi-

versity, consistently lampooned State College President John A. Hannah. In Palo Alto, California, the *Peninsula Observer* was founded and staffed by Stanford University graduate students. It played a large role in focusing attention on ROTC, the Stanford Research Institute (SRI), and the University's connection with big business and the United States Government. The *Observer* ceased publication in November 1969 when the editors decided they were not reaching enough people.

Campus conditions have changed enormously since the 1964 free speech movement at the University of California at Berkeley, and much of the underground press on campus evolved as a reaction to those changes. Over 50 underground newspapers speak to the college community, while the High School Independent Press Service estimates 500 high school mimeographed sheets circulate irregularly on or near high school campuses. UCLA journalism professor Samuel Feldman conducted a 1968–69 survey of 400 high schools in Southern California and discovered 52 of them producing underground publications. Projecting the 12½ per cent of the schools with underground papers in that study upon the 26,098 United States institutions listed in the *1968 Digest of Secondary Schools* would indicate closer to 3,250 such papers than HIPS' estimate of 500, although it is unlikely that the proportion would hold up outside the large urban areas. Most of the editors of these papers would consider it unethical to hold a position in America's technological society, and they take issue with administrations that regard placing graduates in such positions as academic accomplishments. Following bitter student protest against Dow Chemical Company recruiting at Indiana University, the underground *Spectator* editorialized, "One of the points raised by the recent demonstration against Dow Chemical concerns the function served by the University in the broader social system." *Spectator* went on to describe Indiana University as:

> a training and recruiting station for the political and economic elite which dominated U.S. foreign and domestic policy.

During the last week two events have dramatized the 'service station' essence of Indiana University. We point first to the lines of conflict drawn within the faculty over the question of how to respond to the Dow demonstration. Ranged on one side are members of departments whose activities are a step or two removed from the industry-servicing task, namely the arts and sciences. . . .

The angry opposition—those calling for stern punitive action —consisted largely of 'academicians' from such departments as business, law, and education, departments whose commitments to academic goals are tenuous and whose ties to economic and political power are more rigorously institutionalized.

Strange that these people feel threatened by a dramatization of the links between the university, industry, and the war.[4]

Peninsula Observer, South End, Spectator and the fifty-odd papers located at or near universities and colleges are usually distributed on campus, often in the student union. Many college administrators feel that policies forbidding distribution of such papers would only prove the suppression the paper's editorials inveigh against.

The United States Student Press Association (USSPA) is convinced that what is happening in America and on American campuses needs explaining. Founded in 1962, the liberal association offers a news service to 400 campus newspapers and 100 large dailies, including the *New York Times*. David Peterson, a former director of the association wrote:

What the campus newspaper covers determines the breadth and importance of campus dialogue among students, between students and faculty, and among other parts of the university. If campus newspapers, by their focus and concerns, begin to indirectly involve larger numbers of students in a fuller examination of social questions and problems, then they are aiding the university in one of its most important tasks.[5]

The development of a social conscience in the underground

press on campuses is merely an extension of a collective student awakening in the 1960s.

Marshall Bloom and Ray Mungo, founders of the Liberation News Service, were both editors of their college papers—Bloom at Amherest and Mungo at Boston University. Bloom had been in line for the directorship of USSPA, and when the job went to Peterson in 1966–67, Bloom joined with Mungo to start LNS.[6] Only a handful of regular college publications subscribe to the SDS-aligned LNS, but many off- or near-campus underground publications subscribe.

More closely related to the high school campus was *FRED*, a Chicago news service founded to "upgrade the content in high school underground sheets." High School Independent Press Service (HIPS), a former New York national high school news service that had 400 subscribers, was tied in more closely with the national high school underground press scene. For a time in 1968–69 (see chapter six) HIPS distributed weekly news packets containing stories of high school uprisings, dress codes, discipline, police arrests, and policies to independent high school papers around the country. As noted above, HIPS folded when the staff decided to concentrate on the *New York High School Free Press*.

FRED, started in February 1969, distributed its 48-page, stapled, mimeographed publication to 250 high school and off-campus underground papers, mostly in the midwest or near Chicago. By mid-1969 *FRED* was the only underground news service addressing itself to the high school underground press, and then it too was forced out of business before the end of the year when the cost of publishing became too expensive.

The high school underground press is in many ways a reflection of the troubles of secondary education around the nation. Students who are fed up with the system and who feel unable to come to a reasonable democratic compromise in matters of self-expression in high school publications produce their own newspapers—off campus and underground. Many of the campus underground sheets surface around election time when the authorized press often doesn't want or is not permitted the privilege of endorsing candidates for student government posts. The attitude of editors was expressed at a San Francisco Bay Area High School Liberation Conference by a young man who would be identified only as "John of the Haight Commune." In a *Good Times* interview, he said,

> High school is used to condition you to boredom, authority and acceptance. You become used to being manipulated so that the system can use you for the next 50 years.[7]

It is quite logical that much of the youthful opposition to American institutions comes from college and high school publications, since that's where millions of young impatient critics are gathered. Raised on television and transistor radios, today's students are urged by parents and teachers to inquire; but when they inquire about issues more relevant than football games or high school dances, the administration often tells them, "We'll take care of that." High school students are as intensely concerned with the Vietnam war, black inequality, and student curriculum as are their brothers and sisters in college, and the high school underground papers show it. The Fox Valley High School *Post Mortem* in Appleton, Wisconsin, "challenges the myths and realities of their town and society;" *Sans Coullotes* of Bronx High School of Science questions racism and poverty in the ghetto and seeks alternative ways of living. Bruce Trigg of the New York High School Union explained this politicalization in an interview with San Francisco *Good Times* staffer Diane Fowler:

> Our earlier demands had been fairly limited . . . demands to abolish dress codes, rules against leafletting, etc. The demands that came out of the teachers' strike were much more political. We're now demanding an end to all disciplinary suspensions and explusions. In New York, 95% of these are black and Puerto Rican. All pigs and narcs out of the schools. Abolish identification cards. End the tracking system, open admissions to colleges, free housing and meaningful jobs for all high school graduates and power to run the schools.[8]

Once students begin to see their schools as bankrupt, sterile bureaucracies and themselves as prisoners, the stage is set for a high school underground paper. The colorful names of high school papers, such as *The Roach, The Finger, Frox, Big Momma* and the *Doormat Dwellers*, are not just silly titles of student sheets. The levity shown in naming the papers often expresses the absurdity of the role in which the editors find themselves. The mixture of serious radical ideology and light-hearted high school humor is the formula used by most high school underground sheets to bring as many students to their side as possible. The attitude of Ann Arbor, Michigan, high school students after publishing one edition of the underground *US* expresses in dramatic language this frustration and ideology:

> The suppression we encountered was frightening. The savage
> in Huxley's Brave New World comments on our situation,
> saying to the Controller, 'You got rid of them. Yes, that's just
> like you. Getting rid of everything unpleasant instead of learning
> to put up with it. Whether 'tis better in the mind to suffer the
> slings and arrows of outrageous fortune, or to take arms against
> a sea of troubles and by opposing end them . . . But you don't
> do either. Neither suffer nor oppose. You just abolish the slings
> and arrows. It's too easy.' We fear the brave new world, we
> fear . . . 'lobotomized' education, especially in this tremendous
> school. The issue which was created with this publication was
> not one of censorship of the Optimist. The school paper is
> possibly the best in the nation. Outside of administrative
> demands on space and content, we do not question its excellence.
> The existence of anti-distribution laws for student literature
> is the major objection. This is a violation of our constitutional
> rights. If this journalistic endeavor [US] is a failure, it can
> easily be forgotten. But, if you or they force us to stop, we are
> all failures. Then, this school, city, and country, and the
> principles they supposedly represent, are lies.[9]

Sue Wilson, 1968–69 editor of the Homestead, California, high school paper told a group of overground high school editors,

"There wouldn't be any underground papers if we were allowed to print the truth. An underground paper is a knife in the administration's back and is usually thrust at conservative administrations." Miss Wilson added that her journalism adviser and administration allowed her paper to print the truth, but she made her point. When students try to express controversial opinions in a law-abiding manner, they often find they are accorded no rights of expression whatever.

A more dramatic account of high school administration repression appeared in a 1969 *Saturday Review* article by Diane Divoky:

> Last year, John Freeburg, a senior at rural South Kitsap High
> School outside of Seattle, Washington, began to edit and publish
> a mimeographed newspaper for students that reflected his own
> opposition to the Vietnam war, as well as to the adult
> Establishment's reaction to long hair. John himself was clean-cut
> in every sense of the word. The son of a commercial airlines
> pilot, a boy who spent summers working with diabetic children,
> he was a principal's dream; a consistent high honor student,
> one of the three chosen by the faculty as 'outstanding students,'
> a student council representative, and ironically, regional winner
> of the Veterans of Foreign Wars 'What Democracy Means to
> Me' contest. Even in getting out his paper, he operated true to
> form, submitting articles to the school administration for
> approval before each issue.
>
> In spite of this, three months before graduation John was
> suspended, and his parents' efforts to have him reinstated by the
> school board proved fruitless. The state Civil Liberties Union
> stepped in and obtained a court order for his reinstatement.
> An ACLU suit on his behalf for damages brought against the
> school district is still pending in the U.S. District Court. It claims
> that John's civil rights were violated; the district's counterclaim
> uses the traditionally unassailable argument that his activities
> were disruptive to school operation.[10]

Most of the high school underground papers are irregularly published mimeographed sheets such as the Los Altos, California,

Like It Is, Baltimore's *Strobe* or Berkeley High School's R.A.P. (Revolutionary Activist Paper). Hundreds of these sloppily-prepared sheets come out whenever an issue is handled in a way unsatisfactory to the activist students who produce them.

The information and news in campus underground publications represents a challenge, not a threat, to educational administrators and journalism advisers alike. That challenge is to accept the questioning of American institutions posed by these young editors. At best they are looking for ways to make their education meaningful. At worst they make unconventional, unprofessional attempts at self-expression. College and high school publications should be tools of amateur journalists who are stretching to become professionals. As students they must learn that freedom of the press is not just idle rhetoric but is truly administrative policy and reality.

12 / Military and Peace Papers

Under the Pentagon Ground

THE CONDITIONS IN A MILITARY SOCIETY ARE VASTLY more restrictive than those in civilian life. The Military is largely a closed society with its own code of conduct, its own judicial system, and its own rules of behavior. Because the sacrifice of personal freedom is thought necessary for the maintenance of discipline, law, and order, the military is more dictatorial than democratic. The military watchword is authority not freedom and American men have served when called in two world wars with no questions asked.

Much of that changed as the unpopular Vietnam war trudged on. Questions were being asked in many quarters. The military world is obviously not the unquestionable entity it once was. During one month in 1969, eight GIs at Fort Jackson, South Carolina, were charged with demonstrating against the Vietnam war, while at the Presidio in San Francisco fourteen were being court martialed for mutiny—they had protested against stockade conditions. Half the senators did not think the Pentagon was right when it said America needs an Anti-Ballistic Missile system, ROTC has been pushed off or downgraded on many American campuses, and the public opposition to the Pentagon mounts as reports of war casualties continue.

The widespread opposition to American military involvement in Vietnam has done much to force a marriage between the civilian peace movement and the rebels within the armed forces. This match is seen most clearly in the anti-military, pro-peace "resistance" press.

Peace movement papers started in New York City, Chicago and Los Angeles while anti-military underground papers began on bases at Fort Dix, New Jersey, Fort Belvoir, Virginia, and Fort Lewis, Washington. There were sixty such papers publishing irregularly but continually on or near U.S. military installations in America and Europe in 1969.

In one sense those who produce military underground newspapers are the most courageous dissenters of any of the anti-establishment press since the military ground they operate under has a far stricter set of "ground rules." Because freedom of the press is not a traditionally accepted right in military as in civilian life, and because the Army has a separate judicial system to put down any trouble that foments among its 3.5-million members, the anti-military underground editors meet vastly greater opposition than their civilian counterparts. Despite this opposition, military and peace papers in late 1969 were being produced sub rosa and distributed with an effectiveness that both alarms and frustrates the Defense Department.

There are five internationally distributed underground antimilitary or peace papers, and the Pentagon has been able to do little to curb their distribution. The *Bond* in New York, *Task Force* and *Ally* in the San Francisco Bay Area, and Chicago's *Vietnam GI* and *Veterans Stars and Strips for Peace*, have subscribers all over the world. The irregularly published *Task Force* has the largest claimed circulation with printings of 100,000, but *Vietnam GI*, the *Bond*, and the *Ally* distribute on a regular monthly basis and are a steadier source of opposition to the military. *Task Force* publishes whenever there is a mass demonstration against the war or the military.

The *Ally* is published by a coalition of academics, civilians, and ex-GIs against the war, and has a foolproof method of distribution. Mailed in first-class envelopes, the 12,000 circulation "anti-war, anti-brass" monthly is hand-addressed to its subscribers within the military. The return address is rotated to further avoid detection. The risk of destroying morale by opening personal mail has been too great for the military, and the *Ally's* distribution thus has broken through the barrier of military mail sorting. A further safeguard for military underground papers is that it is a violation of Army regulations to withhold personal mail.

Just as in the civilian youth movement, the anti-military GI movement has its schisms—a split between the ultra-left militant wing, another wing that the militants scornfully call "The Trots" (short for Trotskyites), and the Independents. The militant wing is exemplified by the American Servicemen's Union (ASU), a group of ex-GIs dedicated to radical action within the military. ASU is run by Andy Stapp, an ex-Army private. His organization produces the *Bond* out of a small office in New York City. Stapp's denunciation of servicemen dying "to perpetuate the power structure" was published in an early issue of the *Bond*:

> Pvt. Andy Stapp demands that servicemen have rights. He says, you must have the right to higher pay, a voice in the conditions under which you work and that there must be racial equality. He says that enlisted men should have seats on court-martial boards and that you should elect your own officers, that you must have all the rights of free men including the right to refuse illegal orders to fight an illegal war—like the one in Vietnam—and that the only way to get these rights is to organize a union of rank and file GI's.
>
> General Earle G. Wheeler, Chrm of the Joint Chiefs of Staff, speaks for the power structure. He demands obedience. He says, you do as you're told no matter what it is. If he orders you to

go to Vietnam and get killed you aren't supposed to ask
questions. It's just your job to die for important people like
him. And they're ready to fight. They're ready to fight to the last
drop of your blood.

He and his kind are the power behind every rotten officer
and non-com.

He says, I and the people that count give the orders, son; you
just do what you're told and shut up about it and say sir when
you're talking to an officer.[1]

ASU lists eight demands, including the rights to refuse to fight in
Vietnam, to elect officers by enlisted men, and to Federal minimum wages for servicemen. Its objectives have been to focus
attention around the confrontations that stem from these demands. Another publication that identifies with the open confrontation wing is *Head-On*, published by ex-Marines from Camp
Lejeune, the North Carolina training station.

The Trotskyites include groups like Veterans and Reservists
Against the War, the Young Socialists Alliance (YSA), and the
draft-resistance-oriented Student Mobilization Committee to End
the War in Vietnam. The "Trots" restrict their opposition to the
war, while the ASU group is opposed to the entire military establishment. The Fort Jackson incident and the underground paper,
Short Times, typify this group and their single-minded objective.
They claim, "The fight isn't against the Army, it's against the
war. The anti-Army approach confuses the issues to a point where
it's easy to be attacked." Aligning themselves with the "Trots" are
Dull Brass at Fort Sheridan, *Counterpoint* at Fort Lewis, and the
newly-formed *GI Press Service*. The latter was started in July 1969,
publishes its twelve-page magazine twice a month, and is produced
by the above-mentioned Student Mobilization Committee. This
news service is distributed free to GI papers and costs $1 a year for
servicemen subscriptions and $8.50 for civilians.

The Independent faction is closer to its civilian Students for a
Democratic Society counterpart and totally distrusts the military
establishment. This group is represented by the powerful and

effectively-written *Vietnam GI*, the *Ally*, and most of the more militantly anti-military papers. By 1970 it plans to start its own press service to be called *FTA Novelties*.

As these organizations help grind out irregularly-published opposition to the war and the Pentagon, the State Department counts the casualties. According to an April 19, 1969, article in *The New Republic*, "GI's Who Question Why," there were more than 53,000 deserters in the year ending June 30, 1968, compared with only 40,000 the year before. The article indicated draft resistance was on the rise, with General Hersey reporting 23,000 draft delinquents and 1,500 Selective Service Act violation cases brought in the last half of 1968, double the figure for a comparable period in 1967. According to the article, pressure on resisters increased proportionately as the average sentence for draft dodging was up from "32 months to 37."[2]

Whatever the ideological differences of the "Trots" and the ASU wing, both oppose the war in Vietnam. All groups encourage the organization of anti-war GI coffee shops, distribution of anti-war leaflets at rallies and at transportation terminals, plus the establishment of military and peace underground newspapers. The coffee shops promote military opposition and operate near U.S. military posts. Some, like Alice's Restaurant on Chicago's near north side, meet civilian opposition and close shortly after they open. Others in Seattle, Washington, and Killeen, Texas, have become watering grounds for military rebels despite local harassment. Oleo Strut (named after the shock absorber on a helicopter) in Killeen, Texas, caters to 100 or more GIs a night and features protesting folk singers, antiwar movies, and sympathetic female companions.

The distribution of anti-war leaflets has been a further means of dissent within the military, and heavy pressure has been brought to punish those caught distributing or reading such literature.

The editing of the heretical military sheets is not without its dangers. Dennis Davis of *Last Harass* at Fort Gordon was given a dishonorable discharge six days before his two-year hitch was up, although he had a perfect service record at that time. Another serviceman, Bruce Peterson, who edited *Fatigue Press* at Fort Hood in Killeen, Texas, received a stiff eight-year sentence for possession of marijuana which most underground editors believe was planted. After two Fort Ord, California, soldiers were sentenced to four years in prison for distributing anti-war leaflets near the base, underground military editors began familiarizing themselves with Army regulations. A February 1969 amendment to Army regulations allows military personnel the same right to read as anyone else, even when the material is critical of the government. If, however, in the mind of the base commander, the reading material constitutes a clear danger to military loyalty or discipline, he can stop distribution of such material. The problem for the military has been the risk of increasing the interest in antiwar literature by banning such literature or by declaring it dangerous.

The extent of the antiwar movement in underground papers is hard to evaluate since many publications are short-lived or irregularly published. Five such papers are internationally distributed and the remaining fifty-five are peace, resistance or base papers. The sixty papers are listed in the Underground Press Directory beginning on page 178 and are keyed with an "M." These publications are distributed on bases, in train, bus, and airport terminals, at GI coffee houses, and through the "unstoppable" distribution network of the United States Post Office.

These papers serve as bulletin boards for dissenting GIs and militant civilians. They carry calendars of demonstration locations, survival information with lawyer's lists, other antiwar literature, where to get antiwar buttons, and even reports on rock music concerts. WIN in New York City published a list of 150 locations for "weekly vigils for peace," and the *Bond* carries stories of racism among the military and arbitrary discipline cases, while underground base papers stay closer to local issues. They are produced off base with the help of college faculty members and students, veterans of World War II, Korea, and Viet Nam, and even a few Army officers sympathetic to the anti-war movement. The military conviction of Captain Howard Levy, the Army physician who refused to train Green Beret medics for Vietnam, was a major focus of anti-war sentiment and the trial was carried in the major military underground sheets. One paper, *Act*, is published in Paris with the address of Jean-Paul Sartre as its source.

There are signs that the Pentagon is hardening its line against such publications but the military reacts strongly to public sentiment. When the fourteen Presidio soldiers received sentences of fourteen, fifteen, and sixteen years for sitting in a circle singing "We Shall Overcome" to protest conditions in the stockade, the incident was reported to the public by the *San Francisco Chronicle*. Two peace demonstrations and several news stories later, Sixth Army Commander General Stanley R. Larsen reduced the sentence of one soldier from fifteen to seven years. Larsen discovered the same day that the sentence had been reduced by the Judge Advocate General in Washington to two years.

Military underground newspapers are beginning to question the gap between acceptable military and acceptable civilian behavior. Our society's divisiveness over the war in Vietnam has begun to creep into the military bases, and Army privates are beginning to ask for the same constitutional rights they enjoyed as civilians and were guaranteed by the Founding Fathers.

The military underground papers are a vehicle for these questions as young graduates move from the high schools and colleges into the military. The gap between the peace movement and the Army rebels has been closed as they join forces to oppose the Vietnam war.

What will happen if the war ends? An editor of *The Ally* in Berkeley, California, says his paper will no longer have a reason to publish. The publishing members of the anti-racist, anti-authoritarian, anti-ROTC, anti-military underground press will do doubt continue to publish as long as they see a need to fill— and can find an audience to read them.

13 / Influencing the Overground

Buying In or Selling Out

*It cannot be far wrong to say that these
youngsters of the middle class seek a life
style that their parents wish they had sought
while they still had time. They are, in that
sense, fulfilling their parents' wishes—and that
alone may explain why middle-aged editors pay
them so much attention.*

—Horizon Magazine[1]

ONE POINT MUST BE REITERATED BEFORE ANY AT-
tempt can be made to describe the way in which the underground
press influences traditional media or the society in which the traditional media operates. That point is that the underground press
is a reaction to, not a cause of, conditions in society.

When the Berkeley *Barb* ran a story about a parking lot being
made into a soccer field by the University of California, three
weeks before the People's Park incident erupted in that city, it
was not the *Barb* story that created the incident as government
officials claimed. It was rather the general tone of an entire community, as a state governor, a university board of regents and a
police establishment, all were increasingly frustrated and incapable
of dealing with a growing subculture of dissatisfied students, street
people, and political activists. Once again, during the chaotic

1968 Chicago Democratic convention, it was not the distribution of a special edition of 50,000 underground *Rats* by Jeff Shero that caused the youthful disruption and bloody clashes in that city. It was rather the totality of a political system whose concern for self-justification and self-preservation made it afraid of the voice of its young, and led it to choose a candidate who would not disrupt the party organization rather than one who would reflect the preferences of its people. The young went to Chicago to be heard. They were attacked by those who could not bear to listen.

The influence of the underground press on the American Establishment has been wielded largely by challenging and questioning that establishment. A 20-year-old radical student whose 1968 income was $350 asked a conservative San Francisco attorney whose income was closer to $35,000, "How do you expect me to provide answers? I have no money, no power, and you won't even let me vote. You should be glad I'm asking the questions."

As millions of young readers begin to participate in college politics, peace demonstrations, and police confrontations, they become tremendously more inquisitive and aware. This alertness often leads to a feeling of being cheated by the mass media, whose purpose seems to be to perpetuate the system rather than to examine it.

When 1,000 students barricaded themselves inside five Columbia University buildings, the American press frontpaged the story. The stories were curiously detached, however, because no overground reporters were inside the buildings. The various overground media reported police arrests, gave analysis from the administration's point of view, and told everything that happened outside the buildings. The underground press had a dozen staffers in buildings and provided the only inside report on the incident. Liberation News Service, the major source of national and international news from the underground, took pictures and sent reams of copy across the country, recounting poetry readings, dancing, and political developments inside Columbia. Overground *Life* magazine bid for some of the 200-odd pictures taken by underground photographers, but

LNS saved them for the more radical *Ramparts* magazine which ran a cover story on the incident. The underground press audience has grown tired of the overground media, often for good reason. During the People's Park incident in Berkeley when 20,000 students marched in a peaceful Memorial Day demonstration, the local Berkeley *Gazette* did everything it could to incite hatred against the marchers. A front-page *Gazette* story reported, "Several persons openly smoked pot, [while] nearby residents reacted with shock and dismay at the goings on."[2] But no pot smokers or residents were identified, and the Gazette completely ignored the significance of the peaceful, authorized demonstration which was largely responsible for Governor Reagan's decision to send the National Guard troops home. Perhaps that is why the daily *Gazette* circulation slipped from 15,503 to 14,299 from 1962 to 1968 while the underground weekly Berkeley *Barb* grew from zero to 60,000 over the same period.

The *Realist* in New York City, the *Barb* in Berkeley, and the *Free Press* in Los Angeles run articles days and sometimes months ahead of their overground counterparts. In Berkeley the *Barb* ran a story on a Friday about the exhorbitant cost of repairs to the residence of University of California President Charles Hitch; the daily San Francisco *Chronicle* ran the story on Saturday. In Los Angeles the *Free Press* was the first paper to analyze the conditions in Watts after the 1965 upheaval, and the *Realist* did a story on concentration camps over a year before national magazines began to follow suit.

The underground press is unique in its freedom from economic pressures since it has little advertising to be threatened. On the other hand, its staffers do have to eat, a fact which gives the underground another opportunity to influence the overground. Many underground writers earn their living from overground publications, which not only supports them, since they receive little or no remuneration from the underground, but it also provides the underground with news sources "inside" traditional media. Such nationally recognized journalists as Ralph J. Gleason, Andrew

Kopkind, and James Ridgeway earn their "daily bread" from over-ground publications while moonlighting underground. Radio news-man Robert Barron edits the colorfully written little underground sheet, *Globe*, in Salinas, California; and Lincoln Bergman, who contributes a last word to this book, directs news for KPFA radio in Berkeley writing poetry and features for the radical *Movement*.

Established book publishing is another big field where under-ground staffers boast many overground titles. Grove Press has produced books by undergrounders or former underground con-tributors and editors, such as Norman Mailer's *Beyond the Law* and William Burroughs' *Naked Lunch*; Random House published James Ridgeway's *The Closed Corporation*, while Jon Grell says that MacMillan advanced him and his fellow *Rat*-staffer, Paul Steiner, $1,000 each to do a book, *Off the Schools*. As noted else-where, William Burroughs writes articles free for *Rat* while he charges major magazines $500 for similar assignments. John Wilcock is preparing an elaborate overground newsletter entitled "Take a Trip" (air, not acid) for American Airlines while he produces his weekly underground *Other Scenes*. Clark Smith teaches European History at San Jose State College as he and his wife spend evenings preparing the militant, military underground *Ally*.

Overground media not only provide economic support for some underground staffers, they also provide a catalyst and voice for many of the activities of the radical youth movement. Allan Katz-man of *East Village Other* remembers, "When I called the guy from *Time* magazine for a press conference in early 1967 there were only a handful of underground papers. Now, two years after they ran the story, there are hundreds of underground papers." Katzman and his youth movement friends, Paul Krassner and Ab-bie Hoffman, set about using the overground media to further their own radical political ends; they call it "using the media to create myths." Hoffman explains this procedure in *Revolution for the Hell of It*, published by Dial Press.

The American press is not the only institution influenced by the new media. Hair and clothing styles, advertising, music, and political developments as well as sex, sports, and education, are all influenced by the cultural revolution expressed on the pages of the underground press.

Long hair and exotic clothing styles are two modes used by the younger generation to assert their individuality and their opposition to authority. Long hair had been stylish on American men for nearly 200 years until World War I, when the short-hair, no-beard style became a symbol of masculinity, identifying male members of the society with the victorious results of that war. Today many young and not-so-young American males wear long hair, handlebar mustaches, and beards as a sign of their rejection of institutional authority and of a value system that accepts the deliberate killing of people. The bearded hippies and the long-haired students tell society, "I challenge both your system and your authority and reject your values." Rebel styles must be more and more extreme to stand out, however, as establishment businessmen in New York City, Chicago, and San Francisco have converted long hair into a fashion fad. Few middle-aged men outside the police or military sport brush cuts; and Joe Namath, the football folk hero, has brought long sideburns and a hairy fullness above the collar into the once cleancut sports scene.

One clothing advertisement urged middle-class, style-conscious males to "meditate in '68" with a then popular Nehru shirt. "Bonnie and Clyde" ties and coats, gold-rimmed glasses, and 1920 touring caps were worn by radical political leaders and underground staffers two years before they were introduced to the middle class by Madison Avenue.

Movement music has also had a major influence on overground life styles. Now the questioning protest music of Bob Dylan and Joan Baez can be found in the record stacks of nearly every middleclass home with record-buying children. The Beatles' song, "Revolution," and Phil Och's protesting lyrics are the collective expresson of a generation that turns on through involvement of rock music and turns off at the anonymity of the big-band sound.

Influencing the Overground   147

The change in sexual attitudes among American youth is another area greatly influenced by the underground press. United States Supreme Court decisions, starting in 1965, have thrown serious doubt on what constitutes obscenity and pornography. Basically the courts have held that obscenity lies in the eye of the beholder, and that nudity itself is not pornographic if it has any socially redeeming characteristics. After those decisions, the *East Village Other*, Berkeley *Barb*, and *Los Angeles Free Press* began running classified ads from people of all ages and sexes frankly seeking partners. Sexual freedom had long been encouraged by members of the Sexual Freedom League, but before the 1965 Supreme Court ruling the promulgation of their ideology was restricted mainly to *Intercourse*, the League's monthly magazine. *Open City* began running "Notes From a Dirty Old Man," *Barb* began Dr. Hippocrates' comments on aberrant sexual problems, and the San Francisco *Oracle* pictured naked couples locked in orgiastic embrace with a psychedelic drawing in the background. Two years later the society and entertainment pages of the San Francisco *Chronicle* were featuring see-through blouses and topless outfits on women. Young people living and sleeping together in communes is another sign of the decline of hypocritical puritan ethics. By 1969 even some bishops of the Roman Catholic Church were openly evading the Pope's stand on birth control, and priests were abandoning celibacy for marriage.

Education is another American institution influenced by the underground press. Free universities, experimental colleges with student instructors, and student-staffed school boards are all proposals that have been introduced on the pages of underground campus newspapers. School administrators are reluctantly permitting student publications the freedom to print the four-letter words introduced to print journalism by the underground press. Traditional students newspapers at Purdue, California, and Kent State Universities have all had their four-letter word battles as student editors have been moved by the spirit of free-form journalism emanating from the near-campus underground press.

All such changes in social mores and urban behavior patterns are closely interwoven with the underground press, but perhaps the greatest influence has been on American politics. The United States Congress and state legislators across the land have spent substantial amounts of time, energy, and money on studying ways to combat youthful unrest. Racial conflicts in Baltimore and Newark, peace demonstrations in New York City and San Francisco, and student riots and rallies just about everywhere, are being studied on all political levels.

The underground press has raised questions about racial inequality, educational sterility, and moral hypocrisy. It has published demands of the Black Panthers, the Third World Liberation, and the Students for a Democratic Society. Such demands are seldom met, but no other communication medium is presenting them with a bias sympathetic to the students, the peoples of the third world, or the Panthers. The underground press does not pretend to provide answers to the questions they raise. They have little of the economic power and, at most, 10 per cent of the circulation enjoyed by their overground brothers in the media.

The influence of the Underground press is felt only when embarrassing questions about poverty, the defense budget, and the quality of life in America are raised frequently and loudly enough that the real powers in American media—the Establishment press —receives and transmits the message to the wider audience. A look at the changes in American advertising, music, dress, sexual behavior, and politics over the last fifteen years indicates that the underground press's message is getting through.

The Future / Where It's Going

14 / The Future

An Educated Guess

It's going to get bigger all the time.
There are going to be more and more papers
that will give people coverage they're not
getting—and will never get—from the daily
papers.

—MARVIN GARSON[1]

THERE IS NO WAY TO GAUGE THE GROWTH OF UNDER-
ground circulation trends across the country except to observe that
each urban region does support a minimum of one such publication
with a circulation of at least 10,000. Five years ago there was virtually no underground press. Today, as we saw in chapter ten, there
are the *Rat* and *Other Scenes in* New York City with 25,000 cir-
lation each, Detroit's *Fifth Estate* with 17,000, *Kaleidoscope* with
editions in Milwaukee, Chicago, and Madison with 40,000, Atlanta's *Great Speckled Bird* with 12,000, Los Angeles' *Free Press*
with 95,000, Berkeley's *Barb* with 85,000, *Black Panther* with
85,000 and Seattle's *Helix* with 15,000. That handful of underground publications alone represents nearly 400,000 circulation.
This by no means implies the underground press is going to increase its circulation accordingly during the next five years. It does
indicate, however, that the underground press is increasingly fill-
ing a gap in American journalism.

The *Distant Drummer* sold less than 300 papers when it started as a monthly in August 1967. In less than two years, nearly 10,000 bimonthly copies were being sold. The Los Angeles *Free Press* grew from less than 5,000 to 95,000 in five short years while increasing its number of pages from four to forty-eight.

Many underground publications have died during this five-year period and as many others have published with wild irregularity. Most notable among the deaths were the San Francisco and Los Angeles *Oracles*, the *Ungarbled Word* in New Orleans, the *Paper* in East Lansing, Michigan, *Open City* in Los Angeles, and *Connections* in Madison, Wisconsin. But while some papers have folded or changed formats, others have moved in to fill the gaps—when John Bryan's *Open City* closed in March 1969, the Los Angeles *Free Press* picked up some of its circulation and two new papers, *Revolution* and *Image*, began publication. There seems to be no end to the supply of energetic young journalists willing and able to stand the rigors and anxieties of underground newspaper publishing.

The pressures of underground publishing do, however, exhaust even the highest energy types. Walter Bowart of *EVO*, Bob Novick and Marvin Garson of *Good Times*, Jesse Kornbluth and Marshall Bloom of LNS, Walter Wells of the *Illustrated Paper*, and Allan Cohen of the San Francisco *Oracle* are just a few of the outstanding underground editors who have dropped out of publishing in the past two years. Problems with printers, financing, advertising, and unreliable staffers drive many talented editors out of the cities and into communal or farm life, while others substitute paying the mortgage for life in the movement.

The patterns of success held forth by the established press are a great temptation to underground editors, and the underground medium as it grows often takes on the characteristics of the overground. With its ad-heavy pages, the *Village Voice* has all but left the underground. Similarly the Los Angeles *Free Press* has become so successful that it has time clocks, strict internal organization, and an office building superior to that of most established weekly publications. A few publications like these have learned the lessons of organization from the established press and as they do, they begin to look like they'll be around for awhile.

As *Kaleidoscope* expanded its midwestern base from Milwaukee to Chicago to Madison, they began to take on the aura of an established newspaper chain. In 1969 *Kaleidoscope* began to distribute its second section to Indianapolis and Minneapolis for insertion in smaller underground sheets, much like the overground inserts. Other underground publishers in Seattle, New York City, and Chicago distribute returns free to run as inserts for high school underground papers as the underground learns to expand and more effectively utilize its energies. In Boston the *Avatar* group has formed a communications center where they produced the *American Avatar* for awhile, as well as records by Jimmy Kweskin's jug band and others, plus a few films. Concert Hall serves as the underground's national advertising representative while the Liberation News Service helps maintain a telex wire service in New York City, Washington, Berkeley, and London. In three years the underground press has developed a reference library, a press association, and conventions for the education of its members, all very much like the overground.

At the Underground Press Syndicate's fifth meeting since its 1967 founding, UPS discussed techniques, distribution, legal restrictions, and advertising, just as the American Newspaper Publishers discuss such problems. They held workshops, distributed instructional literature, and had their own brand of entertainment—rock music—during a four day convention at Ann Arbor, Michigan. Plans for the future include the establishment of an underground daily, a broadcasting network, cable TV, journalism workshops for beginning underground staffers, and some organized pressure to be applied to the establishment press to encourage its cooperation in preserving the constitutional guarantee of press freedom for underground and overground alike.

Plans for a hippie daily are taken seriously by underground editors around New York City. John Wilcock of *Other Scenes* ran the following story in June 1969:

There is a more or less untapped community in New York City—hip, artistic, creative, radical young—large enough to sustain a new kind of daily newspaper. Such a newspaper, really more of a daily newsmagazine, can be started and continued for a fraction of what professionals usually believe would be needed. At a rough estimate, $50,000. Enough to begin such a paper and operate it five days a week for a period of about three months, which will be long enough to see if it will be a success.

The paper will be printed offset in color (in colored inks and/ or overlays) and sell for 10¢. It would be a morning paper competing on the stands with the New York Times and the Daily News and beginning with an initial circulation of 10,000 copies daily which will at least triple within the three-month period.

The paper will be half-size tabloid, 16 pages, printed on newsprint or possibly a slightly heavier white stock and will be concisely edited and full of pictures and various graphics.

It will not attempt to compete with the regular daily papers in wholesale coverage; its coverage instead will be selective and lean more heavily to features although current (radical) events would be its mainstay and raison d'etre.

It will be a UPS paper and as such will have the cooperation of all 60 papers in the Underground Press Syndicate whose staffers and contributors will all be informed of the paper's start and will cooperate with the regular coverage and features from their various areas.

Apart from an editor, one full-time reporter and one full-time photographer in New York, the paper will rely on numerous part-time and outside contributors to fill its pages. It seems essential to have other regular inflows of material and as the regular wire services (UPI, AP, Reuters, etc.) are too predictable possibly another source should be set up. In my opinion this should be via telex links to other existing radical papers: the Los Angeles Free Press, Berkeley Barb or San Francisco Express-Times seem the most suitable in this country; Oz, the Black Dwarf, It might be best in London. One link to the coast plus possibly one link to Europe would provide ample coverage, supplemented with telephone reportage from radical correspondents in all areas. Most of these people would initially be unpaid. LNS or similar radical press services will also be an essential link.

The paper will appear five times each week and tentative make-up will be: pages 1 and 16 are BOTH front pages, usually pictorial; pages 14 and 15 are FREE CLASSIFIED ADS, two other pages are the responsibility of the advertising department to fill with free ads to deserving people or organizations in the movement when unsold: two pages are the responsibility of the COLUMNIST OF THE DAY (five rotating movement names) two other pages are for the various features, foreign reports, rock coverage, underground movie columns, etc., etc., leaving four pages for the major news, features, or comment of the day. Daily coverage will be very selective; the editor assigning the reporter and/or photographer to the major event(s) of interest to our particular audience. By late afternoon it will be obvious which stories of the day are to get the prominence and the paper would be basically set and laid out in the first part of the evening.

It seems essential to have as much of the production means under one roof as possible to ensure no holdups; ideally the typesetting (already operated efficiently by Other Scenes), make-up; photography dark room and processing; negative and plate making will all be owned by the paper and in the same building. Hopefully a cheap press could be owned by the paper and also on the premises. Failing this, time could be booked with a printer at mid-night each day to run off the already made plates. The paper will appear five mornings a week—Monday thru Friday.

Serious investors are invited to contact John Wilcock, Rm. 419, 41 Union Sq. W., NYC, 10003.[2]

The problems of reaching hippies or other late-rising members of the New York hip culture with a morning paper, or persuading many of the TV- and film-oriented generation to read anything at all, were unanswered in the plan. However, when interviewed in June 1969, Wilcock said he had financial backers for the daily and expected to proceed.

Editorially, we have seen, the underground press seems to swing pendulum-like outwardly to radical politics and inwardly to spiritual and cultural introspection. When the swing retreats from radical politics, as it seemed to after the chaotic 1969 SDS convention in Chicago, the radical papers soften their line. Jeff Shero, editor of the radically political *Rat*, was discussing the future of his paper when it developed that radical American politics included a passion for ecology. Shero exclaimed, "The country is getting the shit ripped out of it; the air is cursed and the water is polluted. We're going to start running articles on noise, pollution, DDT, and corporate farming."

When the swing to radical politics began in the 1967 Vietnam summer, *Helix* in Seattle, *Kaleidoscope* in Milwaukee, and *Distant Drummer* in Philadelphia shifted from psychedelic drawings, rock music, and astrology to anti-police, anti-government, and confrontation politics. In 1969 those papers once again swung inward toward more cultural topics like rock music, alternative life styles, communal living, and survival information for alienated readers.

Madison's *Kaleidoscope* published a manifesto toward a new culture, proposing a movement that would flow from the lives of their readers. The article said, in part.

American capitalism says graduate and leave; we want $10 million to build a community; American capitalism says tear down the Co-op for a Left Turn lane; we say tear down all the left turn lanes, all the used car lots . . . in one night of frenzied dadaistic energy, plant trees, flowers, make Madison beautiful . . . We want the feel of life in a young girl's sweatshirt and jeans, not the feel of death on the dashboard of an Olds . . . we will throw off the yoke of oppression. We will have poets in our drugstores and supermarkets . . . and we will have workers control, students control, womens control, lovers control and childrens control. We need to found a Left which speaks to each corner of our existence, A MARXISM OF EVERYDAY LIFE, an understanding and self-perception of every wheeze of existential desperation, every half-smile of satisfaction of our meager pleasures, every movement of our tepid and boring days. We need a Left which can speak to our dream-fantasies and

MAKE THEM COME TRUE, *a Left which can energize our
visions into social* ANTI-BLUEPRINTS *for the release of
people's spontaneous Goodwill. We need a Marxism which can
fully penetrate the mysteries of the Sick Minds of America,
from Richard Madhouse Nixon to Angst Emory and the paranoid
delusions of grandeur in the Little Men to whom the present
dictators appeal. It is not enough to call the 'leaders' reactionary;
we must have a pathology of total accuracy and prepare an
antidote for remnants of disease in the masses of people. It is
not enough to Overcome and Repress: we must show all the
world why the dictators must be controlled for their own
protection and for the protection of all the people.[3]*

The underground press is largely a reaction to conditions in
American society, but that does not mean it has no visionaries or
prophets. Early issues of the San Francisco *Oracle* were almost
blueprints of the American youth movement for the following
three years. Articles on the Age of Aquarius, the coming of revolutionary rock music, and the confirmation of McLuhan were
set down well before anyone had heard of the musical, "Hair,"
the recordings of Big Brother and the Holding Company, or the
medium being the message. Psychedelic *Oracle* art announced the
coming of the Grateful Dead: "In the land of the dark the ship
of the sun is driven by the Grateful Dead;" Astrology as the religion of the flower children: "This is the Aquarian Age—the age of
the brotherhood and universality of man;" and McLuhan as the
prophet of the electronic generation: "McLuhan embarrassingly
manages to explain pop, op, and camp art, the pot and acid ex-
plosion, and especially what we keep on calling rock and roll."

Fringe underground contributors like Allen Ginsberg, William
Burroughs, and Gary Snyder were outlining the move to consciousness expanding drugs, new sexual freedom, and a withdrawal
from the cities long before the mass magazines got around to
covering such developments.

The past lies dead and forgotten for the NOW generation who
will produce the underground papers of the 1970s. Young people
tell us hopefully "today is the first day in the rest of your life" as

they seek to build a future in an age when America glories in her flights to the moon while she turns her back on poverty in the south and in the cities.

The underground press will continue to question a society whose major media seems unwilling or unable to ask the necessary embarrassing questions about American values and American life styles. The underground press is fifteen years old and like any fifteen year-old in American society, it is uncertain of its future. At the Fifth Underground Press Syndicate meeting in Ann Arbor, Michigan, one editor likened the underground press to "300 fingers." He argued that the Underground Press Syndicate had to work "to make those fingers into a fist." The fist has long symbolized a weapon with which fighting men attack—the hand, a symbol of helpfulness. If those 300 underground papers are going to become a fist it will be because American society has frustrated, alienated, and angered those young journalists to a point where they feel forced to fight.

As this book was being completed, the Underground Press Syndicate was launching a 1970 campaign to find protection from police and government harassment and to gain effective freedom of the press. The campaign was scheduled to contact the American press, journalism education associations, and foundations interested in preserving press freedom. If that support is gained, American journalism will get a badly-needed hand from the underground press. Otherwise those 300-odd papers will continue to join together to form a fist—a fist directed at the sickness middle America tries to conceal from itself.

Each underground newspaper has, in its own way, lent its strength to the continuing battle to improve the quality of American life, questioning where others turn their backs and shedding light where otherwise there might have been darkness. The modern American underground press—with all its cultural and political faces—has provided the only consistent radical critique of fundamental American institutions. It has been a watchdog press. And it will not go to sleep.

Last Word From Underground

Lincoln Bergman and
Allan Katzman

Two TYPES OF NEWSPAPERS PREDOMINATE IN THE modern underground press. Broadly speaking they can be called radical political papers and radical cultural papers. This book has been introduced by a scholar of the field, and now an outstanding editor from each type of paper has been invited to have the last word. The editor of the cultural paper, Allan Katzman, of New York City's *East Village Other*, is a poet and has been a major figure in the development of the underground press as a national movement. Lincoln Bergman, whose paper is one of the radically political ones, is an active journalist and news director for Berkeley, California's listener-supported radio station KPFA. He is also a contributing editor to the San Francisco-based, politically-oriented newspaper, *Movement*.

By Lincoln Bergman

Why go underground? Because there ain't no room for movement overground. Why an underground newspaper? Because the truths they tell cannot be told in the mass media, because they serve needs that are not being served, because a generation in rebellion and facing repression needs a voice.

Many artists have crouched down into the underground foxhole to make effective use of their artistic weapons, in order to stand apart from financial or political tyranny over thought and action, in order to comment on the battlefield around them. The concentration camp. The prison. The insane asylum and the prisons they are hidden in. Poverty. Physical and mental exploitation and oppression. The language and culture of oppression and revolt far more vital than the dying language of the oppressor. The outcast, the stranger, the alienated, the visionary, the practical revolutionary. The criminal underworld. An artist walking down these mean streets finds the insight, anger, and compassion, with which to describe the societies of which these things are wastelands, the guts, and the seeds of the new.

Artists crossing established lines of morality and sexuality, reviling established religion. Writing satire piercing in its irreverence, shock and exposure. Finding ways to describe societies which hide love and sex behind closed doors of fear and inhibition, behind myths of frigid impotence that live a lie happily ever after. And they tell you everything will be cool if you just brush with ultra sheen, with its new special ingredient DDT.

This book contains interviews with many representatives of the underground press, each person with different reasons for involvement, different interests, but they all went underground, because, this nation, in rebellion and facing repression, needs a voice. Because there ain't no room for movement overground.

Underground papers are part of a movement for change. Aware that human duty is not only to destroy, but also to build. That destruction of empty institutions and values of this society is not only a negative task, but a positive one, involving a hope and a belief in the future.

There is no set pattern. There are, instead, many spurts, many ideas, a whole complex of activity, and underground papers are only one part of the whole. And the whole includes the building of political organization, culture, experiments in the future. It includes trends that sometimes scrape against each other as the movement struggles to survive.

Running through the stream of American history is a search for community. The whole includes the communes that begin in cities and in the countryside, those which fail and those which last a while. The whole includes political collectives which seek to use common knowledge and practice to advance more effectively the movement for change. Many underground papers are now based on communes or collectives.

The whole includes the use of techniques devised by the technical genius of advanced industrial society, and yet it tries to take those advances and use them in a different way. Not the idiot images of television, but images that stand out, that attract, that are symbols of meaning in a society whose theorists are fond of saying that the medium is the message.

It includes the use of vital language. The main original contribution of the United States to world culture is in fact the culture of the black people that the United States enslaved. The underground press and the movement use that language. The language seeks originality, descriptive metaphor. Always the language and the images are picked up by the mass media . . . but just as often the language changes so as to avoid being cheapened and bought by powers above it.

It includes attempts to conceive and build alternative institutions that speak to people's needs, needs that are not now being spoken to, or that can only now be satisfied by the selling of one's beliefs, the selling of one's labor power to men whose business is war.

There are tensions within the underground. Drug culture, individualism, mysticism clash often with politics, with the understanding that relative freedom and privilege is based on denial of freedom to other peoples, with the material facts of life around us.

The greatest danger to the underground is repression and the taking over of the form but not the substance of resistance by the overground. The underground fights the takeover by constant change, by making clearer and clearer that its position has to be the destruction of the overground, by increased confrontation and deepening of revolutionary consciousness.

But it is, after all, an underground. Money is needed to survive. Individuals get caught up into images of individual, not group success. The phone is tapped, agents infiltrate the group.

And so the only chance for survival is expansion. The need to speak to more people's needs. The attempt to reach and learn from the people on the bottom . . . who are the people who have the power to make basic change.

There are now underground papers inside the Army. There are papers directed toward a wider audience. Papers that are trying to learn to speak of alternatives, to break down the brainwash that the people of this country have been subjected to for years.

Success cannot be judged now. Success can only be judged on what actually happens in the future, on how well the underground press and the movement for change speaks and fills the crying needs of the people of the world.

But while there are huge problems, and while it is easy for participants to despair, already the movement of which the papers are a part has spoken so strongly that there is little doubt of its effect on people's thinking say, about the war in Vietnam, or the war against black people in this country. Another measure of effect is the need of the mass media and its masters to try and bring the underground within the establishment, to use the trappings of the culture on TV, to try and undercut the strong feelings of revolt which shake this nation. And to try, if all else fails, to crush the men, women, and ideas which the underground expressed.

Enough said. The people whom the writer of this book talked with speak for themselves. The book catches in midflight a rapidly moving stone from David's sling. May the aim be true.

A Blow of your finger on the drum unleashes all sounds and begins the new harmony.

One step of yours is the arising of new men and their marching forward.

Your head turns away: the new love! Your head turns back—O the new love!

'Change our lots, annihilate the plagues, starting with time, sing these children to you.' 'Breed no matter where, the substance of our fortunes and of our wishes,' people beg you.

Arrival from forever, you will go away everywhere.

—To a Reason
Arthur Rimbaud

In the beginning was the Word.

How else to define a point in consciousness where it all begins? The significance of any event needs a time and a place as defined by the laws of language itself. But laws are meant to be broken, and the significance of the Underground Press is, it broke every law that the Word had established.

Basically the significance of the Underground Press is over and no amount of radicalizing its importance by calling it the *Revolutionary Press Movement* will change how it all began.

It has all been a continuous event without Father or Mother, and yet issuing from one Being who is as potent as both. What is underground has to come up. That is the invisible role of Art, and the first rule of History. In Nature, it has always been so, and in Nature nothing begins or ends that is not already there. It takes a wise man to know that, if he ruled the world, everything would be as before. *And God saw the light, and that it was not always so.*

I am not going to name names or tell stories, but simply state that it all began, in America, everywhere and at the same time. It started with people of *high* purpose (I use the word *high* in all its various connotations) working at a level of concentrated energy, and all plugged-in to the consciousness of their Time.

Last Word from Underground   165

The effect of the Underground Press has been more than all its parts. It has established a true concern for events, people, and things, and, at the same time, revolutionized the presentation of information.

These two significant aspects alone are sufficient enough to make it the most important Gospel since the word began. But newspapers are not mere Gospel or just "good news." They are, at their most optimum level, gossip exaggerated with a great degree of intensity.

In a country like America all living experience is reduced to a commodity. To tell people that peace is profitable and practical, pleasure, healthy and productive, that change was the way it was and drastically necessary amounted to heresy.

The message was simple: We'd all better learn to live with each other before there's an empty space in the Universe where the planet earth used to be. God was ruling the world and we'd better learn quick how he was choosing the dials.

In the beginning the Underground Press was Holy. It rallied people around an experience which was not being related to them through accepted forms of communication such as radio, TV, newspapers, and periodicals. And, at the same time, it beckoned people to that experience without rules or stipulations. It coalesced whole groups, separated by sometimes only the distance of their nose, into communities and convinced them they were not crazy or alone. It turned the tables on the Big Boys (establishment and related media) and made masses of young and old alike conscious of a new reality.

The Underground Press changed the format of newspapers, relating it to the visual level of instantaneous recognition, and took the language of objective journalism and raised it to a level of heightened awareness.

TV was more of a progenitor for Underground newspapers because it made available graphic techniques to the Newspaper form which, when utilized correctly, created a fresh and vital approach to the format of "Newspaper." These are the things the Underground Press has achieved in its short lifetime. What is has not achieved is another story better left to the author.

As it now stand, the Underground Press has laid its foundation and the missionary work is just beginning. All over America, in small towns and large, on or near high school and college campuses, young people are putting out or attempting to put out their own underground newspapers. Every day I receive letters from such people asking me for advice. All the letters seem to convey this same message:

DEAR MR. KATZMAN:

  To get straight to the point, we want to start an underground newspaper.

  We are two high school students living in a small South Carolina town. We are concerned about and want to help the uninformed people of Greer (our thriving little town) realize what goes on outside our sealed "dome," especially the young people.

  Since we are completely in the dark, we desperately need advice about starting and running our newspaper, and since you are a well known paper we thought you could help us. Any advice or suggestions you may have for us would be greatly appreciated. Keep in mind our paper must be kept very small for capital is at a minimum.

  We need special help on layouts, organization and just putting the paper together, so could you possibly send us an old copy or recent edition of your paper?

  THANKS.

                                                        BILLY SLOAN
                                                        MARK SMITH

To all these people, I send as many back copies as I can with the same advice: "Do It."

By late 1969 the Underground Press had been taken over by the type of radicals I call, noncreative second-raters. They are the radicals who believe in what they say, and woe to anyone who does not believe accordingly.

But the future holds its own solutions and intelligence dictates recognizable forms and, if not, devours them. In a very short time, the Underground Press will erupt to the forefront of communications in this country. It will be brought there less by a radical commitment to some abstract principles than by a radical commitment to the various and sundry experiences of living. It will have done the things necessary for change without, hopefully, blowing itself and others apart to do it.

It takes a prophet as well as a politico to achieve such ends. It will take an army of poets together to recognize that nothing really important happened today: There were no wars, rapes, or mass murders. No one was carted off to the madhouse, howling and screaming. No one jumped off the Brooklyn, Golden Gate, or any other bridge. No one died in an airplane, car, bus, or train accident. And where everything was found on a rare day when nothing was dying as usual. And—oh yes—where no newspapers failed.

Notes

*All uncredited quotes are derived from
personal interviews or letters.*

1—An Overview

1. Carl Sandburg, "Prairie," *Selected Poems of Carl Sandburg,*
edited by Rebecca West (Harcourt, Brace & World: New York City,
1926), p. 84.

2. Jacob Brackman, "The Underground Press," *Playboy,* August
1967, p. 151.

3. Tom Forcade, "The Underground Press Loves You," *Orpheus,*
August 1968, p. 18.

4. Michael Lyndon, "The Word Gets Out," *Esquire,* September
1967, p. 168.

5. "Student Activists: Free Form Revolutionaries," *Fortune,* January 1969, p. 108.

2—Historical Perspective

1. Judith Greenberg, "An In-depth Study of the Underground
Press of the 1960s," an unpublished term paper, University of Michigan, 1968, p. 16.

2. Brackman, p. 96.

3. Brackman, p. 96.

4. Paul Krassner, "Where the *Realist* is At," *Realist* (No. 82),
September 1968, p. 3.

5. "Every Woman Secretly Wants To Be RAPED," *Open City* (No.
89), February 28–March 6, 1968, p. 3.

6. "Barb Sold," Berkeley *Barb* (Vol. 9, No. 3), July 16–24, 1969,
p. 4.

7. Greenberg, p. 2.

8. "Prophecy—Declaration of Independence," *S. F. Oracle* (Vol. 1, No. 1), September 20, 1966, p. 12.

9. Brackman, p. 152.

10. "Black Panther Party 10-Point Program," *Black Panther*, June 7, 1969, pp. 21–22.

11. "Why do we think we have seen something before, when we have not?" *Chicago Seed* (Vol. 3, No. 11), June 1969, pp. 12–13.

12. "What Is The Underground?" *Avatar* (Vol. 1, No. 1), June 9–22, 1967, p. 6.

13. Mel Lyman, "To All Who Would Know," *Avatar* (Vol. 1, No. 1), June 9–22, 1967, p. 13.

14. "We recognize our old friend," *The Old Mole* (Vol. 1, No. 1), September 13, 1968, p. 1.

15. "Reporters Self-Criticism in Chicago," *Time* magazine, March 21, 1969, p. 71.

3—The Graphic Revolution

1. "The New Media," *S. F. Oracle* (Vol. 1, No. 1), September 20, 1966, p. 2.

2. Ethel Romm, "Psychedelic by Offset," *Editor & Publisher*, November 11, 1967, p. 68.

3. Romm, p. 70.

4. "Generation Gap Marks Press War," *SF Sunday Examiner & Chronicle*, July 13, 1969, Section A, p. 15.

5. "Notice," *Other Scenes*, June 21–23, 1969, pp. 1–20.

6. Thorne Dreyer, "Every day millions," *Liberation News Service*, March 1, 1969, p. 14.

4—Youthful Unrest

1. Bob Dylan, "Blowin' In The Wind," *Bob Dylan's Greatest Hits*, Columbia Records, New York City, 1967.

2. Diane Divoky, "The Way It's Going To Be," *Saturday Review*, February 5, 1969, p. 84.

3. "Foolosophy of Flower Children," *Other Scenes*, December 28, 1968, p. 24.

4. "Music, The Children of Change," *Kaiser Aluminum News* (Vol. 27, No. 1), Spring 1969, p. 25.

5. Anthony Schillaci, "Film As Environment," *Saturday Review*, December 28, 1968, p. 12.

6. John Kenneth Galbraith, *The New Industrial State* (Signet Books: New York City, 1968), pp. 248–50.

7. Michael J. Spencer, "Why Is Youth So Revolting Nowadays?" *Wilson Library Bulletin*, March 1969, p. 647.

5—RADICAL POLITICS

1. John Fitzgerald Kennedy, "An Address to Latin American Diplomats," The White House, March 12, 1962.

2. Margaret Mead, "Youth Revolt: The Future Is Now," *Saturday Review*, January 10, 1970, p. 25.

3. Ernest Dunbard, "Vanguard of the Campus Revolt," *Look* (Vol. 32, No. 20), October 1, 1968, p. 25.

4. "What Is SDS?" *The Old Mole*, June 13–30, 1969, p. 4.

5. "What's With the Women," *The Spectator*, July 1, 1969, p. 7.

6. Liberation News Service, "Women and the Underground Press," *The Spectator*, July 29, 1969, p. 15.

7. Marvin Garson, "Nothing Lasts," *Good Times*, June 4, 1969, p. 16.

8. Kenneth Keniston, *Young Radicals* (Harcourt, Brace & World: New York City, 1968).

Lewis Feuer, *The Conflict of the Generations: The Character and Significance of Student Movements* (Basic Books: New York City, 1969).

6—UNDERGROUND PRESS SERVICES

1. Tom Forcade, "The Great Media Conference," *Wendre Media Newsletter*, September 1969.

2. Allan Katzman, "Underground Press Syndicate," *East Village Other*, June 15, 1966, p. 2.

3. John Sinclair, "I am the Americong—comments on the Papers," *Underground Press Directory*, 1968, p. 24.

4. Ethel Romm, "Inside Report," *Editor & Publisher* (Vol. 101, No. 19), pp. 12, 82.

5. "Dear HIPS . . .," *High School Independent Press Service* (packet No. 11), February 10, 1969, p. 1.

6. "Table of Contents" *FRED*, The Socialist Press Service (Vol. 1, No. 18), June 16, 1969, p. 1.

7. "Monthly Report," *Vocations for Social Change*, March–April 1969, p. 4.

8. G. I. Press Service (Vol. 1, No. 2), July 10, 1969, pp. 1–16.

9. Forcade, "The Underground Press Loves You," p. 28.

7—Economic Operation

1. "Friend of Fascists," *Berkeley Fascist* (Vol. 1, No. 1), June 1969, p. 2.

2. "Barb Sold," pp. 1, 4.

3. "Admen Groove on Underground," *Business Week*, April 12, 1969, p. 84.

4. Ibid., p. 86.

5. Jack Angleman, *The Underground Press* (Ram Classics: M-T Publishers: Las Vegas, Nevada, 1969), p. 147.

6. *Advertising Rates and Schedules*, Underground Press Syndicate, 24 pp., no date.

7. *SDS lit list*, A Newsletter, Chicago, Illinois, 1969, p. 2.

8—Editorial Content

1. Tom Hyman, "Walter Bowart, Mild-Mannered Editor of a Great Metropolitan Newspaper, Fights a Never-Ending Battle for the Liberation of the Human Spirit," *Avant-Garde*, March 1968, pp. 25–31.

2. S. B. Rudnick, "A Fifth Estate," *Orpheus*, August 1968, p. 23.

3. Stew Albert, "Try Them In The Streets," Berkeley *Barb* (Vol. 8, No. 20), May 16–22, 1969, p. 14.

4. Mike Hodel, "On Radio," *Open City*, December 27–January 2, 1968, p. 2.

5. Sheila Golden, "The Perversion of the Legal System," *Other Scenes* (Vol. 3, No. 6), June 1–14, 1969, p. 5.

6. Gaye Sandler Smith, "The Underground Press in Los Angeles," an unpublished master's thesis, University of California, Los Angeles, 1968, pp. 119–123.

7. Ibid.

8. Classified Ads, *East Village Other* (Vol. 4, No. 34), July 23, 1969, pp. 21–22.

9. John Wilcock, "Phoney Facts," *Other Scenes*, June 1–14, 1969, p. 14.

10. Burton Wolfe, "Dr. HIPocrates, Will Bull Sperm Grow Hair On Me?" *Cavalier*, April 1968, pp. 38–40, 63–64, 73–74.

11. Joan Didion, "Alicia and the Underground Press," *Saturday Evening Post*, January 13, 1968, p. 14.

12. John Kronenberger, "What's Black and White and Pink and Green and Dirty and Read All Over?" *Look* (Vol. 32, No. 20), October 1, 1968, p. 21.

13. Gary Allen, "Underground for Adults Only," *American Opinion*, December 1967, p. 4.

14. Forcade, "Underground Press Loves You," p. 18.

15. "The Groupies and Other Girls," *Rolling Stones* (No. 27, February 15, 1969, pp. 11–26.

16. Marty Glass, "What's News," *Dock of the Bay* (Vol. 1, No. 3), August 18, 1969, p. 4.

17. "Table of Centents," *Liberation News Service* (Issue 17), June 12, 1969, p. 1.

9—LANGUAGE ANALYSIS

1. James Baldwin, "As Much of the Truth as One Can Bear," *The Writer's Job* (Scott, Foresman: Glenview, Illinois, 1966).

2. Ralph J. Gleason, "The Times They ARE A-Changin'," On The Town, *San Francisco Chronicle*, August 19, 1968, p. 43.

3. Bob Abel, "Comix of the Underground," *Cavalier*, April 1969, p. 88.

4. Classified Ad, *Los Angeles Free Press* (Vol. 7, No. 2), January 9, 1970, p. 21.

5. "Mailer, McLuhan, and Muggeridge: On Obscenity," *The Realist*, October 1968, p. 6.

6. "Every Woman Secretly Wants To Be RAPED," (front page photograph), *San Francisco Express Times* (Vol. 2, No. 7), February 18, 1969, p. 1.

7. Paul Krassner, "A Speech, Dialectics of Liberation," *Realist* (No. 81), August 1968, pp. 4–5.

8. Rudnick, p. 23.

9. Chester Anderson, "Notes for the New Geology," *S. F. Oracle*, February 1967, p. 2.

10—AUDIENCE ANALYSIS

1. "What Is The Underground?" *Avatar* (Vol. 1, No. 1), June 9–22, 1967, p. 6.

2. Richard Stone, "The Underground Press Succeeds by Intriguing Rebels and Squares," *The Wall Street Journal*, March 4, 1968, p. 1.

3. "The Disobeyers," *Newsweek*, January 13, 1969, p. 81a.

4. Thomas Pepper, "Growing Rich on the Hippies," *Nation*, April 29, 1968, p. 570.

5. Stone, p. 1.

6. Stuart B. Glauberman, "The News From Underground," an unpublished paper, p. 4.

7. Jesse Kornbluth, *Notes from the New Underground*, (The Viking Press: New York City, 1968), introduction, p. xiv.

8. Forcade, "The Underground Press Loves You," p. 28.

9. "What Is The Underground?" *Avatar* (Vol. 1, No. 1), June 9–22, 1967, p. 6.

11—UNDERGROUND ON CAMPUSES

1. Divoky, p. 89.

2. Mary F. Byun, "The Underground Newspaper: A Faculty Member's View," *Student Life Highlights*, May–June 1969, p. 3.

3. James L. Brann, "The Changing Student Press: Underground Papers Vie With 'Regulars'," *The Chronicle of Higher Education*, August 12, 1968, pp. 4–5.

4. Brann, p. 4.

5. Brann, p. 4.

6. Brann, p. 4.

7. Diane Fowler, "School Is Revolting," *Good Times* (Vol. 2, No. 31), August 14, 1969, p. 3.

8. Fowler, p. 4.

9. Divoky, p. 89.

10. Divoky, p. 89.

12—MILITARY AND PEACE PAPERS

1. Andy Stapp, "Demands," *The Bond*, January 1968, p. 2.

2. "GI's Who Question Why," *The New Republic*, April 19, 1969, p. 5–6.

13—INFLUENCING THE OVERGROUND

1. Plumb, J. H., "The Hippies," *Horizon* (Vol. 10, No. 2), Spring 1968, p. 6.

2. "Wild Party After March," *Berkeley Gazette*, May 31, 1969, p. 1.

14—THE FUTURE

1. Pepper, p. 570.

2. John Wilcock, "Hippy Daily Being Planned'," *Other Scenes*, June 1, 1969, p. 15.

3. "Manifesto: Toward a New Culture," *Madison·Kaleidoscope*, (Vol. 1, No. 1), June 23–July 6, 1969, p. 4.

Glossary of Terms Used in the Underground Press
(*Including the Classifieds*)

ACAPULCO GOLD: the finest grade of marijuana, from Mexico

AC/DC: bisexual; especially with regard to couples who swap partners for both heterosexual and homosexual activity

ACID: LSD (a hallucinogenic drug, lysergic acid di-ethylamide)

AUNT: an older homosexual man who wants to take care of a younger man

BAG: one's vocation and/or avocation

BAIL OUT: to leave while you can, before you are wiped out

BEAUTIFUL: general expression of approval; especially for anything that is nonEstablishment

BENT: slightly upset by someone's behavior

BUMMER, *or* BUM TRIP: nightmarish effects during use of hallucinogenic drugs; generally something undesirable

BREAD: money

BROWNED OFF: exasperated or upset by someone's behavior

BUG OUT: to leave, often in a hurry

BURNED: to have money stolen or to have been cheated

BUSTED: arrested

BUTCH: masculine

CHICANOS: Mexican-Americans

COKE: cocaine

COOL: socially acceptable person or behavioral trait

COP OUT: to change one's values to conform with societal norms for a selfish purpose

DIG: to intensely approve of something or someone, or of someone's ideas

DISCIPLINE: whipping, or other sadistic-masochistic activities

DRAG: a boring person or experience

DROP OUT: to cease to live by established societal norms

EDGE CITY: a place where people live dangerously

175

ESTABLISHMENT   everybody outside the underground movement; people who run the country and/or approve the status quo

FALL OUT: to go into a semi-coma after a methedrine trip; to go to sleep

FEDS: members of the federal narcotics squad

FLOWER PEOPLE: hippies

FREAK OUT: to lose control or inhibitions, often through the use of drugs, music, or meditation

FRENCH LESSONS: offering or seeking cunnilingus or fellatio

FUCKED OVER: harassed or molested, usually by police or authorities

GAY: homosexual

GOGGLERS: homosexuals, homophiles

GRASS: marijuana

GROOVY: a highly acceptable person or experience

HANG-UP: a person's psychologically weak area; a nuisance

HAIRY: a very tense or uncomfortable experience

HAPPENINGS: sexual, social, or spontaneous activities

HEAD: a person who uses psychedelic drugs

HEAD SHOP: a place where "heads" meet and purchase psychedelia

HEAVY: a very serious idea or experience

HIGH: a good trip

HOLDING: a person possessing illegal drugs

JOINT: a marijuana cigarette

LEATHER: suggesting "disciplinary" sado-masochism

LID: one ounce of marijuana

THE MAN: the police

MOTHERFUCKER: a person who is against the radical political movement

NARC, NARK, NARCO: a member of the federal narcotics squad

PIG: a member of the police force

PISSED: angry

POT: marijuana

PUT-ON: deception; to convince somebody that something untrue is true

RAP: to speak freely

RIPPED OFF: to have been taken advantage of

RIGHT ON: in good psychological condition

RUN: the continuous use of methedrine for a week or longer

SCENE: a place where "in" or "hip" people meet for an event

the SCENE: general cultural atmosphere (middle-class scene, rock scene)

SMACK: heroin

SPEED: methedrine (methamphetamine hydrochloride), stimulating to the central nervous system. It accelerates body metabolism, hence its name.

SPEED FREAK, METH MONSTER: one who takes massive doses of methedrine

SPLIT: to leave

SPLITTERS: to quit the movement

STRAIGHT: of the Establishment

STP: a psychedelic drug more potent than LSD. It produces up to four-day trips

STONED: under the influence of heavy drugs

SWINGER: one who leads an active and varied sex life

SWITCHES: indulging in bisexual activity

TUNE IN: to revise one's personal views regarding societal norms after "enlightenment" through a psychedelic experience

TRIP, TRIPPING: to be under the influence of drugs

TURN ON: to become hypersensitive to oneself and one's environment, often through the use of psychedelic drugs

UP FRONT: paid in advance

UPTIGHT: tense, or holding rigidly to Establishment values

VIBRATIONS: what one senses about something (either good or bad)

WIPE-OUT: a disaster, as in surfing when one's surboard is overturned

ZONKED-OUT: exhausted; to be useless, as if drugged or drunk

ZAPPED: to have been cheated

Directory of Underground Newspapers

T HE UNDERGROUND OR PSEUDO-UNDERGROUND PUBLICA-
tions listed here are as complete a roster of American underground
newspapers as could be compiled at publication time. This list is a
compilation of several limited directories, plus approximately 100
underground publications not listed in any directory.

The swift pace of events which characterizes underground journalism
makes it impossible to offer a complete or current listing. As this last
was being put together at least fifteen underground papers were being
started and an equal number were ceasing publication. Some of the
papers listed are no longer publishing, but have published within the
past twelve months. Because of the highly irregular publishing sched-
ule of high school underground sheets, no effort has been made to include the estimated 3,000 papers in this category.

Students of the underground press and American librarians
interested in the phenomenon should establish contacts with the Underground Press Syndicate, Post Office Box 26, New York City 10014,
where the most up-to-date list will be maintained.

The list below is coded with a "C" for college or campus publications, "M" for military or peace papers, "BL" for black, and "CH" for
Chicano newspapers.

Abas, Newark, New Jersey
About Face, Fort Pendleton (M)
Aboveground, Ft. Carson (M)
Activist, Oberlin, Ohio (C)
Adult Reporter, San Diego, California
Advocate, Los Angeles, California
Aerospaced, Grissom AFB (M)
A Four-Year Bummer, Chanute Air Force Base (M)

Agape, San Francisco, California
Agitator, Lynchburg, Virginia
Aim, New Haven, Connecticut
Alaska Free Press, Fairbanks, Alaska
Albany Liberator, Albany, New York
Alchemist, Manhattan, Kansas
Alice, Blacksburg, Virginia
The Ally, Berkeley, California
Alternative, Naperville, Illinois
Altus, Atlanta, Georgia
Anarchos, New York City, New York (CH)
Ann Arbor Argus, Ann Arbor, Michigan (C)
Anvil, Durham, North Carolina
Appleton Post Mortem, Appleton, Wisconsin (C)
Aquarius, Berkeley, California
Arcane Logos, New Orleans, Louisiana
Argo, Santa Barbara, California (C)
As Is, Washington, D.C.
As You Were, Fort Ord (M)
Astro Projection, Albuquerque, New Mexico
Asterisk, Omaha, Nebraska
Atlanta Cooperative News Project, Atlanta, Georgia
Atlantic Sun, Boca Raton, Florida
Attitude Check, Camp Pendleton (M)
Avatar, Boston, Massachusetts
Avalanche, Berkeley, California
Avalanche Undermine Press, Berkeley, California
The AWOL Press, Fort Riley (M)
Axon, Portland, Maine
Balloon Newspaper, Santa Cruz, California
Baltimore Free Press, Baltimore, Maryland
Bandersnatch, Tucson, Arizona (C)
Bauls of the Brickyard, West Lafayette, Indiana
Bayonet, Presidio of San Francisco (M)
Berkeley Barb, Berkeley, California
Berkeley Fascist/People's Paper, Berkeley, California
Berkeley Monitor, Berkeley, California

Berkeley Tribe, Berkeley, California
Big Stink, Plattsburg, New York (C)
Big Us, Cleveland, Ohio
Black and Red, Kalamazoo, Michigan
Black Fire, San Francisco, California
Black Mask, New York City, New York (BL)
Black Observer, Camden, New Jersey (BL)
Black Panther, Oakland, California (BL)
Black Politics, Berkeley, California
Blacksburg Free Press, Blacksburg, Virginia
Blade, The, Oshkosh, Wisconsin
Block Print, Providence, Rhode Island (C)
Bolinas Hit, Bolinas, California
Bond, The, New York City, New York (M)
Bowditch Review, The, Berkeley, California
Bragg Briefs, Fort Bragg (M)
Bridge, Chicago, Illinois
Brief Candle, Ames, Iowa
Broadside, Los Angeles (M)
Broadside, Boston, Massachusetts
Buddhist Junkmail Oracle, Cleveland, Ohio
Buffalo Chip, Omaha, Nebraska
Buffalo Insighter, Buffalo, New York
Bullsheet, Storrs, Connecticut
California Digest, Santa Barbara, California
California Sun, Los Angeles, California
Campaigner, The, New York City, New York
Campus Resource, St. Louis, Missouri (C)
Campus Underground, Cedar Falls, Iowa (C)
Capitalism Stinks, Berkeley, California
Capitol East Gazette, Washington, D.C.
Caw! New York City, New York
Center Cinema Coop, Chicago, Illinois
Changes, San Rafael, California
Chessman, The, Fort Beaufort (M)
Chicago Journalism Review, Chicago, Illinois
Chispa de Revolution/Spark, San Francisco, California (CH)
Cocktail Hour, Oberlin, Ohio (C)

Columbia Free Press, Columbia, Missouri (C)
Commitment, Stanford, California (C)
Common Ground, Los Angeles, California
Common Sense, Springfield, Massachusetts
Communication Company, Corte Madera, California
Connections, Madison, Wisconsin (C)
Conscientious Objector News Notes, Philadelphia, Pa. (M)
Counterdraft, Los Angeles, California (M)
Counterpoint, Stevens Point, Wisconsin (C)
Counterpoint, Fort Lewis (M)
Crocodile, Gainesville, Florida
CSM: Chicano Student Movement, Los Angeles, California (CH)
Crusader Newsletter, From Exile
Daily Meadow Muffin, New York City, New York
Daily Planet, The, Bellingham, Washington
Daily World, New York City, New York
Dallas Notes, Dallas, Texas
Damascus Free Press, Damascus, Maryland
Deserted Times, Berkeley, California
Despite Everything, Berkeley, California
Dialogue, Hayward, California
Digger News Family, San Francisco, California
Dock of the Bay, San Francisco, California
Douglaston Free Press, Douglaston, New York
Drum, Brooklyn, New York
Duck Power, San Diego, California (M)
Dull Brass, Fort Sheridan (M)
Dwarffe, Phoenix, Arizona
East Village Other, New York City, New York
Electric Newspaper, Salt Lake City, Utah
Electric Rainbow, Santa Barbara, California
El Gallo, Denver, Colorado (CH)
El Grito Del Norte, Espanola, New Mexico (CH)
El Ma Criado, Delano, California (CH)
El Papel, Albuquerque, New Mexico (CH)
Experimental College Press, San Jose, California (C)
Extra, Providence, Rhode Island
Eyes Left, Travis AFB (M)

Fatigue Press, Killeen, Texas (M)
Fed Up, Ft. Lewis (M)
Feiaferia, Altadena, California
Fifth Estate, Detroit, Michigan
Firing Line, Chicago, Illinois
First Issue, The, Ithaca, New York (C)
Flag-In Action, Fort Campbell (M)
Florida Free Press, West Palm Beach, Florida
Fluxus West, San Diego, California
Forum, Crawfordsville, Indiana
Freak, San Francisco, California
Free Kazoo, Syracuse, New York (C)
Free City News, San Francisco, California
Free News, Chicago, Illinois
Free Press, Cambridge, Massachusetts
Free Press Underground, Columbia, Missouri
Free Student, Berkeley, California (C)
Free University Cosmic, Columbus, Ohio (C)
FTA (Fun, Travel & Adventure), Fort Knox (M)
Fort Lauderdale Free Press, Ft. Lauderdale, Florida
Free Venice Beachhead, Venice, California
Free You, The, Palo Alto, California
F.T.E. (Fuck The Establishment), Hollywood, California
Fusion, Boston, Massachusetts
GAF, Barksdale AFB (M)
Gambit, Tempe, Arizona
Gig Line, Fort Bliss (M)
GI Voice, New York City, New York (M)
GI Organizer, Fort Hood (M)
Glebe, Greenfield, California
Gnosis, Portland, Oregon
Good Times, San Francisco, California
Gothic Blimp Works, New York City, New York
Granpa, New York City, New York
Grass Roots Forum, San Gabriel, California
Great Speckled Bird, Atlanta, Georgia
Greenfeel, Carmel, California
Green Revolution, Brookville, Ohio

Gregory, Columbus, Ohio (C)
Grinding Stone, Terre Haute, Indiana
Guardian, New York City, New York
Guerrilla, Detroit, Michigan
Haight/Ashbury Maverick, San Francisco, California
Haight/Ashbury Tribune, San Francisco, California
Hair, Minneapolis, Minnesota
Hard Core, The, New York City, New York
Hard Times, Washington, D.C.
Harry, Baltimore, Maryland
Head, Boston, Massachusetts
Head-On, Camp Lejeune (M)
Helix, Seattle, Washington
Heresy II, Ft. Leonard Wood (M)
Heterodoxical Voice, Newark, Delaware
Hinky-Dinky Report, San Diego, California
High School Free Press, New York City, New York (C)
Horseshit, Hermosa Beach, California
Huachuca Hard Times, Sierra Vista, Arizona (M)
Hundred Flowers, The, Lexington, Kentucky
Iconoclast, Santa Monica, California
Idler, Washington, D.C.
Illustrated Paper, Mendocino, California
Image, Los Angeles, California
Indiana Liberal, Indianapolis, Indiana
Indian Head, Santa Ana, California
Independent Eye, Yellow Springs, Ohio
Inner City Voice, Detroit, Michigan
Innysfree, Cambridge, Massachusetts
Inquisition, Charlotte, North Carolina
Instant News Service, Berkeley, California
Institute For the Study of Non-Violence Journal, Carmel, California
Intercourse, San Francisco, California
Iowa Defender, Iowa City, Iowa
Jewish Currents, New York City, New York
John Brown Speaks, Berkeley, California
Jones Family Grandchildren, Norman, Oklahoma
Journal of the Resistance, Boston, Massachusetts

Kaleidoscope, Milwaukee, Wisconsin
Kaleidoscope, Madison, Wisconsin
Kaleidoscope, Chicago, Illinois
Kandie Kansas, Lawrence, Kansas
Karma, Saginaw, Michigan
Katz, Katz, Brayns & Braun, Alliston, Massachusetts
Kept Press, Palo Alto, California
Kiss, New York City, New York
Kudzu, Jackson, Mississippi
Lancaster Free Press, Lancaster, Pennsylvania
Laputa Gazette, Urbana, Illinois
La Raza, Los Angeles, California (CH)
Last Harass, August, Georgia (M)
Le Chronic, Roxbury, Massachusetts
Left Out, Peoria, Illinois
Left Face, Ft. McClellan (M)
Leviathan, New York City, New York
Liar, St. Petersburg Beach, Florida
Liberation, New York City, New York
Liberator, The, Ames, Iowa
Little Paper, Los Angeles, California
Logistic, Fort Sheridan (M)
Long Beach Free Press, Long Beach, California
Long March, The, Baltimore, Maryland
Looking-Glass, The, Ann Arbor, Michigan
Looper, The, (Calif. National Guard) San Francisco, California (M)
Los Angeles Free Press, Los Angeles, California
Love, Reno, Nevada
Love Street, San Francisco, California
Lux Verite, West Lafayette, Indiana
Marine Blues, Treasure Island, California (M)
Mama, New York City, New York (C)
Mark Twain Column Piss, Boston, Massachusetts
M-Cup News, Minneapolis, Minnesota
MDS Newsletter, New Orleans, Louisiana
Mega Middle Myth, Beloit, Wisconsin
Middle Earth, Iowa City, Iowa
Middle Eye, Riverdale, California

Militant, The, New York City, New York
Milwaukee Courier, Milwaukee, Wisconsin
MindFucke, Washington, D.C.
Minneapolis Free Press, Minneapolis, Minnesota
Minority of One, Passaic, New Jersey
Miscellaneous Man, Los Angeles, California
Modern Utopian, Berkeley, California
Montana Free Press, Denver, Colorado
Monthly Review, New York City, New York
Mother of Voices, Amherst, Massachusetts (C)
Motive, Nashville, Tennessee
Movement, The, San Francisco, California
MDS (Movement For A Democratic Society), New York City, New York
Moving Times, Chicago, Illinois
Mountain Free Press, Denver, Colorado
Nacla Newsletter, New York City, New York
National Underground Review, New York City, New York
Neged Hazerem, New York City, New York
New England CNVA, Voluntown, Connecticut
New England Free Press, Roxbury, Massachusetts
New England Resistance, Boston, Massachusetts
New Haight/Ashbury Free Press, San Francisco, California
New Hard Times, Highland Park, Illinois
New Left Notes, Chicago, Illinois
New Patriot, The, Ithaca, New York
New Politics News, New York City, New York
News and Letters, Detroit, Michigan
Newsoundpaper, New York City, New York
New South Student, The, Nashville, Tennessee
News From Nowhere, DeKalb, Illinois
News Project, Flushing, New York
New University Conference Newsletter, Chicago, Illinois
New University Thought, Detroit, Michigan (C)
New York Avatar, New York, New York
New York Herald Tribune, New York, New York
New York High School Free Press, New York City, New York
New York Peace & Freedom Party, New York City, New York (M)

New York Review of Sex, New York City, New York
New York Roach, Great Neck, New York (C)
NMA&M Conscience, Las Cruces, New Mexico (CH)
Nola Express, New Orleans, Louisiana
Non-Paper, Missoula, Montana (C)
North American Congress on Latin America Newsletter, New York City, New York
Northwest Passage, Bellingham, Washington
Notes From Underground, San Francisco, California
Nueva Mission, San Francisco, California (CH)
Oberlin Other, Oberlin, Ohio (C)
Obligore, The, New York City, New York (M)
Ojus Sun, Ojus, Florida
Old Market News, Omaha, Nebraska
Old Market Press, The, Paducah, Kentucky
Old Mole, Cambridge, Massachusetts (C)
OM, Pentagon, Washington, D.C. (M)
Omega Press, Corpus Christi, Texas
Open Cell, Oakland, California
Openings, San Francisco, California
Open Door, Milwaukee, Wisconsin
Open Process, San Francisco, California (C)
Open Ranks, Fort Holabird (M)
Open Sights, Fort Belvoir (M)
Oracle, Mill Valley, California
Organ, Fresno, California
Orpheus, Phoenix, Arizona
Other Scenes, New York City, New York
Our Daily Bread, Minneapolis, Minnesota
Outlaw, San Quentin Prison, California
Overflow, Ann Arbor, Michigan (C)
Paperbag, Los Angeles, California
Paper Highway, Schenectady, New York
Paper Tiger, Boston, Massachusetts
Pawn, The, Frederick, Maryland (M)
Peace & Freedom News, Berkeley, California (M)
Peace Brain, Chicago, Illinois (M)
Peace & Freedom News, Baltimore, Maryland (M)

Peacemaker, Cincinnati, Ohio
Peace Pipe, San Bernardino, California
Peninsula Observer, Palo Alto, California (C)
People Yes, The, Columbus, Ohio
Philadelphia Free Press, Philadelphia, Pennsylvania (C)
Phoenix, Nashville, Tennessee
Pith, Milwaukee, Wisconsin (C)
Pittsburg Point, Pittsburg, Pennsylvania
Plain Truth, Champaign, Illinois
Plain Wrapper, Palo Alto, California (M)
Planet, San Francisco, California
Pleasure, New York City, New York
Position, San Francisco, California
Prism, Princeton, New Jersey
Prisoners' Information & Support Service, Boston, Massachusetts
Probe, Santa Barbara, California (C)
Protein Radish, North Carolina
Psychedelic Review, New York City, New York
Pterodactyl, Grinnell, Iowa (C)
Punch, Worcester, Massachusetts
Quicksilver Times, Washington, D.C.
Quixote, Madison, Wisconsin
Radical America, Madison, Wisconsin
Radical's Digest, New York City, New York
Radical Education Project Newsletter, Ann Arbor, Michigan
Radicals in the Professions Newsletter, Ann Arbor, Michigan
Rag, Houston, Texas
Raisin Bread, Minneapolis, Minnesota
R.A.P. (Revolutionary Activists Paper), Berkeley, California
Rat, New York City, New York
Realist, New York City, New York
Rebirth, Phoenix, Arizona
Rebirth of Wonder, New York City, New York
Reconstruction Press, Topeka, Kansas
Red Eye, San Jose, California
Red Guard Community News, San Francisco, California
Resist, East Palo Alto, California
Resistance, Stanford, California

Resistance Press, Chicago, Illinois (M)
Revolution, San Diego, California
Rip Off, Berkeley, California
Rising Up Angry, Chicago, Illinois
Roach, The, Honolulu, Hawaii
Roach, Eau Claire, Wisconsin (C)
Rolling Stone, San Francisco, California
Roosevelt Anarchist, Chicago, Illinois
Rough Draft, Tidewater Area (M)
Round Peg, San Antonio, Texas
Salaam, Nyack, New York
Salty Dog, Philadelphia, Pennsylvania
San Diego Free Door, San Diego, California
San Diego Free Press, San Diego, California
San Jose Maverick, San Jose, California
San Francisco Free Press, San Francisco, California
Sattva, Sarasota, Florida
Scimitar, Ithaca, New York (C)
Screw, New York City, New York
Screw, Lawrence, Kansas
SDS Newsletter, Athens, Georgia
SDS Newsletter, Terre Haute, Indiana
SDS Newsletter, New Orleans, Louisiana
Searcher, The, Wellesley, Massachusetts
Second City, Chicago, Illinois
Second Look, New York City, New York (C)
Seed, Chicago, Illinois
Serve The People, Carmel, California
79¢ Spread, The, Carmel, California
Shaft, Tempe, Arizona
Shakedown, Wrightstown, New Jersey (M)
Sherwood Forest, Newport Beach, California
Short Times, Fort Jackson (M)
Silent Planet Speaks, Minneapolis, Minnesota
SNCC Newsletter, Atlanta, Georgia
Sons of Jabberwock, San Jose, California (C)
South End, Detroit, Michigan (C)
Southern Patriot, Louisville, Kentucky

Space City Times, Houston, Texas
Spartacus, Fort Lee
SPD (*Special Processing Detachment*) *News*, Fort Dix (M)
Spectator, Bloomington, Indiana (C)
Spectrum, Washington, D.C.
Spirit, Nashville, Tennessee
Spokane Natural, Spokane, Washington
SSOC Newsletter, Charlottesville, Virginia
St. Louis Free Press, St. Louis, Missouri
Street News, Toledo, Ohio
Strike Back, Fort Bragg (M)
Student Mobilizer, New York City, New York (C)
Student Times, Inc., Boston, Massachusetts (C)
Student Voice, New York City, New York (C)
Sun, Ann Arbor, Michigan
Sun, Detroit, Michigan
Sunflower, Richmond, Virginia
Sun/Trans Love Energies, Detroit, Michigan (C)
Symposium Press, Framington, Michigan
Task Force, Berkeley, California (M)
Teaspoon Door, La Mesa, California
Technocracy, Rushland, Pennsylvania
Teleoscopic Collage, Denver, Colorado
TET Offensive, The, New York City, New York (M)
Third Floor, The, Boston Massachusetts (C)
Thrust, The, Pittsburgh, Pennsylvania
Top Secret, Fort Devens (M)
The Toy, Los Angeles, California
Treason, New York City, New York
Tri-Continental Information Bulletin, New York City, New York
Truth Instead, Treasure Island (M)
12th Street Rag, Milwaukee, Wisconsin
UFO, The, Columbia, South Carolina
Uhuru, Oakland, California (BL)
Ultimate Weapon, Fort Dix (M)
Ungarbled Word, New Orleans, Louisiana
Underground, Arlington, Virginia
Underground Oak, Oakland Naval Station (M)

Universal Communications, San Francisco, California
University of Hartford News/Liberated, Hartford, Connecticut (C)
Upcountry Revival, Knoxville, Tennessee
Up Front, Los Angeles, California
Vanguard, San Francisco, California
Veritas, Boonton, New Jersey
Vets Stars and Stripes For Peace, Chicago, Illinois (M)
Vibrations, Phoenix, Arizona
Vietnam GI, Chicago, Illinois (M)
Viet Report, New York City, New York
View From Here, Baltimore, Maryland
Virginia Community-Media Project, Charlottesville, Virginia
Vocations For Social Change Newsletter, Canyon, California
Voice of the Women's Liberation Movement, Chicago, Illinois
Voice of the Turtle, San Diego, California
Vortex, Lawrence, Kansas
Walrus, Urbana, Illinois
Walrus, The, Austin, Texas
Warren Forest Sun, Detroit, Michigan
War Resistors League, New York City, New York (M)
Washington Free Press, Washington, D.C.
Water Tunnel State College Free Press, State College,
   Pennsylvania (C)
Western Activist, Kalamazoo, Michigan
West Virginia Free Press, Institute, West Virginia
Willamette Bridge, Portland, Oregon (C)
Wildcat Report, New York City, New York
WIN, New York City, New York (M)
Wind and Chaff, New York City, New York
Woods, The, St. Mary-Of-The-Woods College, St. Mary
   of the Woods, Indiana
Wretched Mess News, West Yellowstone, Montana
WYSO News, Yellow Springs, Ohio
Xanadu, St. Louis, Missouri
Yellow Dog, Berkeley, California
Your Military Left, Fort Sam Houston, Texas (M)
Zippies, Evanston, Illinois

ates / *The following plates eproduce selected pages from underground papers to illustrate some aspects of their design and content.*

PLATE 2

e art and a hand-drawn caption get the message across on e back page from the Washington Free Press *(February -28, 1969). The border and the word "Unite!" are printed yellow and make the page an effective poster. [Printed th permission of the* Washington Free Press*]*

PLATE 3

derground papers are unconcerned with cramming as ny words and stories as possible into a given space. The ulting freedom from conventions of newspaper makeup llustrated in this front page from Boston's Avatar *nuary 19–February 1, 1968). [Printed with permission* Avatar*]*

PLATE 4

e of op-art and screening techniques make the man's ad, taken from a photograph, seem to float upward on s front page. The original was printed in a bleed of red d blue inks to illustrate the theme of Indian wisdom for issue of the San Francisco Oracle *(February 1967). It o illustrates the willingness of the underground to oordinate details like the title of the paper, price, and blication date to overall design. [Printed with permission the* Oracle*]*

PLATE 5

king type talk in the news columns of the underground ss is demonstrated by this page of the San Francisco *acle (February 1967, p. 10). The body type was set on a ritype machine and pasted into the spaces of the drawing. erground publishers would find it economically unrealistic handle feature material so elaborately. [Printed with mission of the* Oracle*]*

PLATE 6

painstaking collage of engravings and drawings conveys n Francisco artist Sätty's vision of a scheduled rock tival. This front page indicates the amount of planning, e, and work invested by the artist and New York editor an Katzman to capture the spirit of a news event for e East Village Other. *[Printed with permission of Sätty]*

PLATE 7

This full-page illustration of a love generation couple locked in embrace demonstrates the uninhibited approach to underground art of the San Francisco Oracle *(February 1967, page 51). The photograph of the couple was superimposed on the pattern of a tablecloth taken from the pad of a hippie artist. The graphic effect was so dramatic that it sold thousands of copies as a poster at $1.50. [Printed with permission of the* Oracle*]*

PLATE 8

This issue of Other Scenes *(June 22–23, 1969) shows how far underground editors will go to avoid the economic and artistic restrictions of old-fashioned newspaper graphics. Sixteen of the twenty pages are blank. [Printed with permission of* Other Scenes*]*

PLATE 9

The Berkeley Barb *often has a heavily inked, overly busy front page. Unconcerned with what the page says, editor Max Scherr tries to make his reader feel the message. Because the message is often ugly, the* Barb *has the dubious honor of being known as "the world's ugliest newspaper." [Printed with permission of the* Berkeley Barb*]*

PLATE 10

Headlines, headlines, who's got the headlines? This page from San Francisco's Good Times *(May 14, 1969) puts groups of four headlines together in pinwheel designs. Ease of reading is sacrificed to visual effect. Such convention-shattering fun is, no doubt, part of the psychic pay for working on an underground publication. [Printed with permission of* Good Times.*]*

PLATE 11

Characteristic of the political cartoons of movement artist Ron Cobb is this dark sketch. Cobb's drawings usually depict America on the brink of destruction. [Printed with permission of Sawyer Press]

PLATE 12

Newspaper comics in the 1930s were concerned with everyday things like getting a job and raising a family. Today's underground comix deal with a different sort of readers' concerns—drugs, sex, and society's taboos. This page by Walt Crowley from Milwaukee's Kaleidoscope *sends up the respectable pornography of automobile advertising and design. [Printed with permission of Walt Crowley]*

HIGH SCHOOL STUDENTS

THE BEST WAY TO EDUCATE ONESELF IS TO
BECOME PART OF THE REVOLUTION — CHÉ

PLATE 3   **193**

194 PLATE 4

SUNBEAR SPEAKS

I am an Indian in blood and in spirit. I wish to tell you about my people. The American Indian had a sense of living and belonging with the land and blending with nature. Because of this, he referred to the animals as his Little Brothers. His sense of responsibility to the land was such that he never killed anything he didn't eat, and when going out to gather a plant for medicine or food, he didn't take from the first plant he saw, but, offering a prayer, he would go to the next one of the species and harvest from it.

The average medicine man has a knowledge of about 150 herbs he uses for treatment of sicknesses and in ceremonies. The sense of giving and being part of the land was such that in farming, he would always give to the land in the form of fertilizer such as fish, and never disturb the topsoil any more than necessary in planting. He left the stumps of trees in his garden and planted around them.

When invaders from across the Great Water tried to force treaties upon my Brothers, and make them sell their lands, their reply was, "The Earth is our Mother. We do not sell our Mother." And such it is, for every living thing receives sustenance from the Earth.

Friends, Brothers, if you wish respect and friendship of the traditional Indians, or other communes with the land, be not like the tourist, but bury your cans and other rubbish, so that the Earth will remain clean to the eye of its keepers.

The American Indians' religion was such that when the first Europeans came to his lodges, the Indian people said, "Come, sit down and have something to eat, Brothers," and gave them gifts. And their way was to treat the stranger as the Great Spirit in disguise. Hospitality was a sacred thing to us. That is why it is a sad thing to come up on the streets of your city and stop someone to say Hello, and their eyes freeze over, and their philosophy is to treat the stranger as the Devil in disguise. "I don't know, so I don't trust him," is their thought.

It is the old way to give food or medicine to one from behind a mask so that he will not feel obligated to the giver, but think of it as a gift from the Great Spirit. It is the way of my people, in the spring when the fish run to spawn, that we spear extra fish and give them to the old people and women without men, so that these may also share the gift of the Great Spirit. The old way in the buffalo hunt was the same. When Crazy Horse killed buffalo, his first buffalo was for the families who had no hunter to get their meal for them.

When a man went to become a chief, he would fast, and say, "What can I do that will best serve my people?" The Indians fasted because at a time when you take no food or water, you are closest to the Great Spirit, and your mind is not dwelling on things of the belly. A man was chief only so long as he did the will of the people. There were cases where a chief got too "chiefy" and arrogant. He would go to sleep at night, but while he slept, the band moved away, leaving him to be chief all to himself.

For many years the

American Indian had neither freedom of religion nor freedom from religion, in that he could not practice his own beliefs, and yet missionaries of all sorts were assigned to his particular reservation. If he didn't attend their churches, he was regarded as a "bad Indian." Chief Joseph, the great Nez Perce wished to follow the way of his people, the Dreamer's religion, but he was forbidden to, and his battles in defense of his people and their way of life is recorded in your histories. Sitting Bull was murdered for standing up for the rights of his people and for following the Ghost Dance religion. Today there are many Indian people who are practicing the old ways still, and others who are returning to learn of them.

The sweat lodges are used by many people to cleanse their bodies and give a sense of feeling with the land. For in this ceremony, one sits naked upon the Earth in an enclosed dwelling with hot rocks in a pit. Sage is first thrown into the pit. Then the rocks are pushed in from outside. Cold water is thrown on the rocks, bringing up steam. The steam sweats the body, cleansing it of poisons. The sweat runs off, back to Mother Earth, and you step forth, a new person, to walk upon the land.

Brothers, learn this. Learn to walk upon the land. Learn a sense of balance and blending with the land. Do (CONT ON PAGE 25)

PLATE 5   195

Vol. 4, No. 34　　　Metropolitan 15¢　　　July 23, 1969

THE east village OTHER

THE WILD WEST

A SAN FRANCISCO FESTIVAL

AMERICAN TANTRIC #2 (YAB-YUM) 51 Available in poster form from Berkeley Bonaparte
PHOTO: PAUL KAGAN P.O. Box 1250 Berkeley, Calif

PLATE 7 197

SPECIAL ISSUE   JUNE 22-30   25 cents

NOTICE

This special issue costs 25 cents.

Most of it consists of blank pages.

Do not waste your money buying it unless
(a)   you want a collector's item, or
(b)   you are planning to enter our do-it-
        yourself newspaper contest.

first prize is $250.

Details in centerfold.

PLATE 9   199

RHYTHM, RIOTS AND REVOLUTION

by Dr. David A. Nobel
350 pages, paper, from Box 977, Tulsa, Oklahoma 74102, $1.

This book is a must for every serious student of revolution, and for a buck, how can you go wrong. Dr. Nobel delineates the depth and savy of the Communist Party's master plan to use Rock & Roll, as well as Folk music, to undermine the morals and traditions of the Good Ol' U.S. of A. It is a pisser and is right up there on the Top Ten of Books for the FBI. You must read this book to believe it. It has a style which is difficult, but understanding the fever and patriotism of the Author, once mastered, will reward the serious student of communism as well as the casual reader.

If you like "Rhythm Riots and Revolution," you'll love the companion volume. "Communism, Hypnotism, and The Beatles." Remember the directive from the Grand Dragon. "Bop Music spreads Communism." KKK.

![star graphic with text: Book Flip, Tap-Tip, Poor Food, Slow Flash]

doc stanley

Here is a way to cut down on the rock and bottle problem which seems to plague our police departments in ghetto areas.

Pay a bounty on rocks—1¢ on little stones, a nickel for a rock, a dime for a half-brick and a quarter for a whole brick. This program operated by the police department with the cooperation of the garbage men, would provide an income for the unemployed youth of the ghetto.

They could collect rocks, stones and bricks and sell them to the police, who would, in turn, cause the garbage men to haul them off to wherever the trash goes. The fact that it would be individual policemen giving out the money for the rocks would improve police community relations.

Everybody loves the paymaster, and treats him with respect, and that's what we need to get the ghetto kids to show the cops—respect.

The rock bounty program would cut down the number of rocks available for social protest.

The bottle problem is a little harder. Glass, especially the new thin no-deposit no-return bottles, is sharp and breakable. The gutters of the slum areas are carpeted with small pieces of glass, produced by broken bottles broken by slum kids. These cut the feet and are a drag to the motorist.

Broken bottles are a hazard. Unbroken bottles are a worse hazard, as these form the basis of the famous Molotov Cocktail which has seen so much use in liberation festivals throughout the world.

Two hazards of the ghetto could be eliminated if the easy-to-get glass bottle could be eliminated. Let's get the beer, wine, soda pop and whicky botlers to get rid of the bottle in the ghetto. Put huge taxes on bottles, to get rid of them.

Make distributing bottles in areas where glass is found on the street a misdemeanor. Pay bounties for bottles turned into police, as in the rock bounty program above.

Require special licenses to engage in the sale of bottled goods. Pay bonuses for plastic bottle development. Get the broken glass and bottles out of the ghetto.

SECRET MESSAGE TO THE PRESIDENT

Dear Dick:

Do you think it would be possible to reopen the Kennedy-King Killings after J. Edgar Hoover retires? A lot of people out our way would have a lot more "faith" in you as a President if you did.

In case you are looking for the proper orders to give to end American Participation in Vietnam, you might want to try these three.

Order number one: Send all the boats to Saigon.

Order number two: Lead all the men onto the boats.

Order number three: Bring all the boats back home.

We are still willing to give you a chance, but your free time is running out. Your guards are getting nervous and that's a bad sign. A worried guard implies problems at the top. You are too new on the job to have made enemies of your own; but you may have inherited some of LBJ's. Look closely at those about you.

Your true blue buddy
A Friend

The County Officials who are depriving the poor in 425 United States Counties of access to food stamps and other forms of food programs are in violation of title 18, sec 241-2 of the United States Code. Why Doesn't the Government Act. They have the law, make them use it.

(Clip this story, sign it, paste it on a post card and send it to the congressman or senator of your choice.)

Poor old Abe Fortas got caught with his hand in the till, to hear some tell it, and now he has got to quit the Supreme Court on account of it. Why doesn't Tom Dodd, who kept his bribe, have to quit the Senate? Anti-Semitism maybe?

What lesson can be learned from Adam Clayton Powell, Abe Fortas, and Tom Dodd.

![star graphic with text: Till Tap, Rock Trip, Wash Out, Live Ones]

We'ed like to give away free subscriptions to our brave boys in Vietnam but the post office demands that our subs be paid for or we fuck up our 2nd class permit. We make an offer of 100 free subs to servicemen for a $300 contribution by a stateside supporter. Any takers, call 863-7775 or if not in service come to 1550 Howard St., S.F. and we'll see what we can work out.

Any time the urge to mess over Safeway or Mayfair crosses your mind why not try a Shop-In? Take your shopping cart and head straight for the grape section. Line the bottom of the cart with fresh grapes. Next lay on heavy fruit cans. Next goes rotted vegetables, you'll find plenty. Pile up all the perishable items you can find. The final step can be to either leave the cart in a back aisle or bring it up to the checker. Let them add it up and split at your own speed. This system is a lot more irritating than a protest line.

Tonight (Thursday) there will be a Rock Concert Benefit for the Daily Gater at Nourse Auditorium, Hayes & Van Ness, SF, from 7 pm to 2 am. Admission is $2. Groups scheduled include: Sons of Champlin, Cold Blood, Cleanliness & Godliness Skiffle Band, Country Weather, Euphonius Wail, Something Else, Tree Wizard, and Band X with lights by Deadly Nightshade. The show is being produced by Gary Jackson of the Matrix, sound by Audio Alley of San Francisco, and Larry the Lion of KMPX will emcee. The Daily Gater has been the student newspaper at SF State for the past 53 years, the recent attempts by the college to prevent it from publishing have failed. The Gater is now publishing independently of the college Administration and this benefit will erase its debts and keep the Free Voice of the press rolling.

Did you see where Highway 80, near Pinole, collapsed? Is this a matter for criminal prosecution against the contractors? If not, why not. The people of California spent good money for those roads and maybe it is time for a good scandle in the State Department of Highways. Is everybody honest there? That would be wonder never before beheld.

Did you see where Hubert Humphrey got his? Outside a pub by a group of anti-war students in England. Do you think he will be able to hold classes in his new job? Or is he under house arrest for life? Didn't LBJ look terrible on TV at the Eisenhower Funeral. His deluxe confinement must be wearing on him, He can only come out on State occasions, never to walk among his fellow men again. Too fucking bad, baby—too fucking bad.

![star graphic with text: Hump Thump, Bust Down, Grape Rape, March Fong]

Isn't March Fong just wonderful. Three Cheers For March Fong. Yeah, Wow March Fong. A great Lady and a Great Assemblywomen.

Political Demand:

One fortyeight-inch aqueduct be sent to Oriaibi.

?????

Why doesn't the high school band play at the next peace march?

Auto-Trichonosis

Android of destruction
Antithesis of creation
May you find damnation
    before the time of your passing
May you wander endlessly
    through the horror
        of your un-self-awareness
    through the cosmic dust
        of your ignorance and fear
    through eternal visions
        of your bestial darmic illusions
May your not-at-oneness become pappable anguish
May you know the pain of a desperately lonely soul
May your non-being find immolation
    in the unconsuming flames
    of the primordial fire
        at the stake of All-being Denied.

Jim Richard
Berkeley

Somebody "dropped a dime" on Chicago SDS and the Fire Department and the Police Department answered in force. The alarms were false but a bunch of SDS Execs were popped for "interfering with an officer." $12,500 bonds @ 10% is $1250 of movement money down the drain, plus the legal hassles and energy tied up for months.

In Chicago the Black People have also used false alarms to bring police and fire authorities into traps where guns and equipment were taken from helpless police and fire trucks damaged. So it is even, baby, ain't it?

PLATE 11 201

a child's garden of ☆PROGRESS☆

CHAPTER THE FIRST—AUTOMOBILE TECHNOLOGY

LONG AGO TRAVEL WAS VERY ARDUOUS AND MEN RODE ANIMALS...

LIKE THIS HORSE

I BELIEVE !!!

CONFESS YOU FILTHY HERETIC

WITH THE INVENTION OF THE WHEEL CAME CIVILIZATION.

THE 19TH CENTURY SAW THE THE ADVENT OF STEAM POWER

THE

THE INTERNAL COMBUSTION ENGINE WAS PERFECTED

THE AGE OF THE CAR DAWNED

THE AUTOMOBILE HAD A DRAMATIC IMPACT UPON WESTERN CULTURE

STOP FOR FOOT TRAFFIC

KAFUMP

AS THE MOTOR CAR EVOLVED TWO (2) BASIC DESIGNS EMERGED PHALLIC (fig.1) AND VAGINAL (fig.2) BOTH BEING EXTENSIONS OF THE HUMAN LIBIDO

CENSORED

fig.1   fig.2

PHALLIC: THE VIRILE P-75 • VAGINAL: The Labia Major

THEN ON THAT FATEFUL DAY... THEY COLLIDED !!!

BOOSH!

PFUT

9 MONTHS LATER...

beep

toot

AND THE FORD SAID UNTO THEM BE FRUITFUL AND MULTIPLY, AND REPLENISH THE EARTH AND SUBDUE

Index

overground press (*cont.*)
attack on news in, 108–10; underground's influence on, 145–49; youth's disbelief in, 53
Ovshinsky, Harvey, 22–23

Paper, 128–29
Pawlock, Victor, 18
peace movement papers, 136–42
Peck, Abe, 27, 73
Peninsula Observer, 30–31, 129
People's Park incident, 37. 99–100, 145
Perdue, Howard, 77
Peterson, Bruce, 141
Peterson, David, 130
Philadelphia Free Press, 31, 33, 37, 63, 65, 128
P. O. Frisco, 23
pornographic papers, 114–15, 122
Post Mortem, 132
press syndicates, 69–79
printing, expenses of, 85; new graphic techniques, 39–49
Progressive Labor Party (PL), 62
psychedelic drugs, 116–18
publishing centers, multiple, 44–45
Pulitzer, Joseph, xvi

radical movement, exploitation by establishment, 8–9; and underground press, 60–68; political vs. cultural emphasis, 98–112, 161
Rag, 63
Rat, 13, 34–36, 46, 63, 93, 144
Realist, 4, 13, 16–17, 116, 121–22, 145
record companies, 8–9, 91
Resist (antidraft organization), 63
Resistance (antidraft organization), 63
Ridgeway, James, 36, 146
Rimbaud, Arthur, 165
rock music, 55, 107, 118–19, 147
Rodriguez, Spain, 102
Rolling Stone, 19, 107
Rolontz, Robert, 91
Romm, Ethel, 40
Rudd, Mark, 62
Rudnick, Bob, 69, 71, 97
Ryan, Sheila, 24

salaries, 93
Samberg, Paul, 34
San Francisco Express-Times, 32–33, 41, 115; *see also Good Times*
San Francisco Oracle, 18, 23–24, 39–42, 45–46, 49, 159
Sandburg, Carl, 3
Sanders, Ed, 25
Sans Coullotes, 132
Sartre, Jean-Paul, 142
Scherr, Max, 20–22, 84–85
Schillaci, Anthony, 56
Schoenfeld, Eugene, 104
Schreiber, Jim, 20
Screw, 93–94
SDS, 61–64, 75–76, 95
Seale, Bobby, 25
Sebela, Terry, 27, 28
Seed, 25, 27–28, 42
Segal, Earl, 25
sex ads, 92, 103, 115
sexual behavior, 103, 104–105, 148
Sexual Freedom League, 148
Shero, Jeff, 34–35, 73, 144, 158
Short Times, 139
Sinclair, John, 70–72
Slater, Paul, 124
Smith, Clark, 146
South End, 127–28
Space City Times, 36
Spectator, 42, 129–30
Speltz, Frank, 24
Spiegelman, Art, 102
Spock, Benjamin, 52
Stamberg, Margie, 24, 66
Stanford University, 30–31, 129
Stapp, Andy, 138
Steiner, Paul, 75, 146
street sales, 89–90
Student Communications Network, 77
Student Mobilization Committee to End the War in Vietnam, 78, 139
Student Nonviolent Coordinating Committee (SNCC), 66
Students for a Democratic Society (SDS), 61–64, 75–76, 95
Stulman, Harriet, 76
subscription rates, 90
subjective reporting, 99–100
Swerdloff, Howie, 75